Poems: New and Old by John Freeman

John Frederick Freeman was born in London on 29th January 1880.

He began his working life as an office boy at 13. Although known as a poet he did, in fact, build an early, successful, career in insurance.

He formed a close friendship with the poet Walter de la Mare from 1907, who, impressed by Freeman's poems spent some time lobbying on his behalf with Edward Marsh and Harold Munro to get Freeman accepted into their Georgian Poetry series. It took time but eventually his work was accepted.

Freeman has been described as "tall, gangling, ugly, solemn, punctilious".

He won the Hawthornden Prize in 1920 with 'Poems' 1909-1920. 'His Last Hours' was set to music by fellow poet Ivor Gurney.

John Frederick Freeman did on 23rd September 1929

Index of Contents

PRESS NOTICES

Mr. Freeman's landscapes have an individuality which entitles him to his own place as a poet of nature.... The appreciation of his lofty ardours, his desolate landscapes and his strange, though beautiful, rhythms and forms of verse, is not one which springs up instantly in the mind; but once it has arisen it does not diminish.—New Statesman.

I think that whatever limitations our age and our poetry may have, Mr. Freeman's poetry, and much else that is now being written, will find in all succeeding generations readers to whom it will give companionship and comfort.—Mr. J.C. Squire, in Land and Water.

This book must be read steadily through; quotation can reveal little of its scope, its richness.... When a man, in poems that are clearly fragments of autobiography, thus surrenders to the world the life of hisspirit, the beauty of what he writes is inseparable from its truth. Truth endures, and a prophet would have a sad foreboding of posterity if he did not believe that of this day's poets Mr. Freeman will not be among the forgotten.—Times Literary Supplement.

This rarefied air is something to which the reader must adjust himself; but he finds the process of adjustment made easy by a peculiar fascination in the atmosphere which Mr. Freeman creates. If it is aloof from ordinary experience, it is by so much the more individual; and in it there are to be found thrills and feelings, an understanding of a particular aspect of nature, which have not hitherto been reported in poetry—Westminster Gazette.

"—He still'd
All sounds in air; and left so free mine ears
That I might hear the music of the spheres,
And all the angels singing out of heaven,
Whose tunes were solemn, as to passion given."

NOTE

With the exception of two or three poems which have appeared in newspapers, or in an anthology entitled Twelve Poets, the verses in the first part of this volume have not hitherto been printed. The second part contains Memories of Childhood and Other Poems, and the third part retrieves many verses from Presage of Victory (1916), Stone Trees (1916), Fifty Poems (1911) and Twenty Poems (1909). Chronological order has not been carefully observed, or avoided, in the arrangement of the third part, but the earlier pieces will easily be distinguished by those who may wish to distinguish them.

PART I

THE EVENING SKY

Rose-bosom'd and rose-limb'd
With eyes of dazzling bright
Shakes Venus mid the twinèd boughs of the night;
Rose-limb'd, soft-stepping
From low bough to bough
Shaking the wide-hung starry fruitage—dimmed
Its bloom of snow
By that sole planetary glow.

Venus, avers the astronomer,
Not thus idly dancing goes
Flushing the eternal orchard with wild rose.

She through ether burns
Outpacing planetary earth,
And ere two years triumphantly returns,
And again wave-like swelling flows,
And again her flashing apparition comes and goes.

This we have not seen,
No heavenly courses set,
No flight unpausing through a void serene:
But when eve clears,
Arises Venus as she first uprose
Stepping the shaken boughs among,
And in her bosom glows
The warm light hidden in sunny snows.

She shakes the clustered stars
Lightly, as she goes
Amid the unseen branches of the night,
Rose-limb'd, rose-bosom'd bright.
She leaps: they shake and pale; she glows—
And who but knows
How the rejoiced heart aches
When Venus all his starry vision shakes;

When through his mind
Tossing with random airs of an unearthly wind,
Rose-bosom'd, rose-limb'd,
The mistress of his starry vision arises,
And the boughs glittering sway
And the stars pale away,
And the enlarging heaven glows
As Venus light-foot mid the twinèd branches goes.

BEECHWOOD

Hear me, O beeches! You
That have with ageless anguish slowly risen
From earth's still secret prison
Into the ampler prison of aery blue.
Your voice I hear, flowing the valleys through
After the wind that tramples from the west.
After the wind your boughs in new unrest
Shake, and your voice—one voice uniting voices
A thousand or a thousand thousand—flows
Like the wind's moody; glad when he rejoices
In swift-succeeding and diminishing blows,

And drooping when declines death's ardour in his breast;
Then over him exhausted weaving the soft fan-like noises
Of gentlest creaking stems and soothing leaves
Until he rest,
And silent too your easied bosom heaves.

That high and noble wind is rootless nor
From stable earth sucks nurture, but roams on
Childless as fatherless, wild, unconfined,
So that men say, "As homeless as the wind!"
Rising and falling and rising evermore
With years like ticks, æons as centuries gone;
Only within impalpable ether bound
And blindly with the green globe spinning round.
He, noble wind,
Most ancient creature of imprisoned Time,
From high to low may fall, and low to high may climb,
Andean peak to deep-caved southern sea,
With lifted hand and voice of gathered sound,
And echoes in his tossing quiver bound
And loosed from height into immensity;
Yet of his freedom tires, remaining free.
—Moulding and remoulding imponderable cloud,
Uplifting skiey archipelagian isles
Sunnier than ocean's, blue seas and white isles
Aflush with blossom where late sunlight glowed;—
Still of his freedom tiring yet still free,
Homelessly roaming between sky, earth and sea.

But you, O beeches, even as men, have root
Deep in apparent and substantial things—
Earth, sun, air, water, and the chemic fruit
Wise Time of these has made. What laughing Springs
Your branches sprinkle young leaf-shadows o'er
That wanting the leaf-shadows were no Springs
Of seasonable sweet and freshness! nor
If Summer of your murmur gathered not
Increase of music as your leaves grow dense,
Might even kine and birds and general noise of wings
Of summer make full Summer, but the hot
Slow moons would pass and leave unsatisfied the sense.
Nor Autumn's waste were dear if your gold snow
Of leaves whirled not upon the gold below;
Nor Winter's snow were loveliness complete
Wanting the white drifts round your breasts and feet.
To hills how many has your tossed green given
Likeness of an inverted cloudy heaven;
How many English hills enlarge their pride

Of shape and solitude
By beechwoods darkening the steepest side!
I know a Mount—let there my longing brood
Again, as oft my eyes—a Mount I know
Where beeches stand arrested in the throe
Of that last onslaught when the gods swept low
Against the gods inhabiting the wood.
Gods into trees did pass and disappear,
Then closing, body and huge members heaved
With energy and agony and fear.
See how the thighs were strained, how tortured here.
See, limb from limb sprung, pain too sore to bear.
Eyes once looked from those sockets that no eyes
Have worn since—oh, with what desperate surprise!
These arms, uplifted still, were raised in vain
Against alien triumph and the inward pain.
Unlock your arms, and be no more distressed,
Let the wind glide over you easily again.
It is a dream you fight, a memory
Of battle lost. And how should dreaming be
Still a renewed agony?
But O, when that wind comes up out of the west
New-winged with Autumn from the distant sea
And springs upon you, how should not dreaming be
A remembered and renewing agony?
Then are your breasts, O unleaved beeches, again
Torn, and your thighs and arms with the old strain
Stretched past endurance; and your groans I hear
Low bent beneath the hoofs by that fierce charioteer
Driven clashing over; till even dreaming is
Less of a present agony than this.

Fall gentler sleep upon you now, while soft
Airs circle swallow-like from hedge to croft
Below your lowest naked-rooted troop.
Let evening slowly droop
Into the middle of your boughs and stoop
Quiet breathing down to your scarce-quivering side
And rest there satisfied.

Yet sleep herself may wake
And through your heavy unlit dome, O Mount of beeches, shake.
Then shall your massy columns yield
Again the company all day concealed....
Is it their shapes that sweep
Serene within the ambit of the Moon
Sentinel'd by shades slow-marching with moss-footed hours that creep
From dusk of night to dusk of day—slow-marching, yet too soon

Approaching morn? Are these their grave
Remembering ghosts?
... Already your full-foliaged branches wave,
And the thin failing hosts
Into your secrecies are swift withdrawn
Before the certain footsteps of the dawn.

But you, O beeches, even as men have root
Deep in apparent and substantial things.
Birds on your branches leap and shake their wings,
Long ere night falls the soft owl loosens her slow hoot
From the unfathomed fountains of your gloom.
Late western sunbeams on your broad trunks bloom,
Levelled from the low opposing hill, and fold
Your inmost conclave with a burning gold.
... Than those night-ghosts awhile more solid, men
Pass within your sharp shade that makes an arctic night
Of common light,
And pause, swift measuring tree by tree; and then
Paint their vivid mark,
Ciphering fatality on each unwrinkled bark
Across the sunken stain
That every season's gathered streaming rain
Has deepened to a darker grain.
You of this fatal sign unconscious lift
Your branches still, each tree her lofty tent;
Still light and twilight drift
Between, and lie in wan pools silver sprent.
But comes a day, a step, a voice, and now
The repeated stroke, the noosed and tethered bough,
The sundered trunk upon the enormous wain
Bound kinglike with chain over chain,
New wounded and exposed with each old stain.
And here small pools of doubtful light are lakes
Shadowless and no more that rude bough-music wakes.

So on men too the indifferent woodman, Time,
Servant of unseen Master, nearing sets
His unread symbol—or who reads forgets;
And suns and seasons fall and climb,
Leaves fall, snows fall, Spring flutters after Spring,
A generation a generation begets.
But comes a day—though dearly the tough roots cling
To common earth, branches with branches sing—
And that obscure sign's read, or swift misread,
By the indifferent woodman or his slave
Disease, night-wandered from a fever-dripping cave.
No chain's then needed for no fearful king,

But light earth-fall on foot and hand and head.

Now thick as stars leaves shake within the dome
Of faintly-glinting dusking monochrome;
And stars thick hung as leaves shake unseen in the round
Of darkening blue: the heavenly branches wave without a sound,
Only betrayed by fine vibration of thin air.
Gleam now the nearer stars and ghosts of farther stars that bare,
Trembling and gradual, brightness everywhere....
When leaves fall wildly and your beechen dome is thinned,
Showered glittering down under the sudden wind;
And when you, crowded stars, are shaken from your tree
In time's late season stripped, and each bough nakedly
Rocks in those gleamless shallows of infinity;
When star-fall follows leaf-fall, will long Winter pass away
And new stars as new leaves dance through their hasty May?
—But as a leaf falls so falls weightless thought
Eddying, and with a myriad dead leaves lies
Bewildered, or in a little air awhile is caught
Idly, then drops and dies.

Look at the stars, the stars! But in this wood
All I can understand is understood.
Gentler than stars your beeches speak; I hear
Syllables more simple and intimately clear
To earth-taught sense, than the heaven-singing word
Of that intemperate wisdom which the sky
Shakes down upon each unregarding century,
There lying like snow unstirred,
Unmelting, on the loftiest peak
Above our human and green valley ways.
Lowlier and friendlier your beechen branches speak
To men of mortal days
With hearts too fond, too weak
For solitude or converse with that starry race.
Their shaken lights,
Their lonely splendours and uncomprehended
Dream-distance and long circlings 'mid the heights
And deeps remotely neighboured and attended
By spheres that spill their fire through these estranging nights:—
Ah, were they less dismaying, or less splendid!
But as one deaf and mute sees the lips shape
And quiver as men talk, or marks the throat
Of rising song that he can never hear,
Though in the singer's eyes her joy may dimly peer,
And song and word his hopeless sense escape—
Sweet common word and lifted heavenly note—
So, beneath that bright rain,

While stars rise, soar and stoop,
Dazzled and dismayed I look and droop
And, blinded, look again.

"Return, return!" O beeches sing you then.
I like a tree wave all my thoughts with you,
As your boughs wave to other tossed boughs when
First in the windy east the dawn looks through
Night's soon-dissolving bars.
Return, return? But I have never strayed:
Hush, thoughts, that for a moment played
In that enchanted forest of the stars
Where the mind grows numb.
Return, return?
Back, thoughts, from heights that freeze and deeps that burn,
Where sight fails and song's dumb.
And as, after long absence, a child stands
In each familiar room
And with fond hands
Touches the table, casement, bed,
Anon each sleeping, half-forgotten toy;
So I to your sharp light and friendly gloom
Returning, with first pale leaves round me shed,
Recover the old joy
Since here the long-acquainted hill-path lies,
Steeps I have clambered up, and spaces where
The Mount opens her bosom to the air
And all around gigantic beeches rise.

THY HILL LEAVE NOT

Thy hill leave not, O Spring,
Nor longer leap down to the new-green'd Plain.
Thy western cliff-caves keep
O Wind, nor branch-borne Echo after thee complain
With grumbling wild and deep.
Let Blossom cling
Sudden and frozen round the eyes of trees,
Nor fall, nor fall.
Be still each Wing,
Hushed each call.

So was it ordered, so
Hung all things silent, still;
Only Time earless moved on, stepping slow
Up the scarped hill,

And even Time in a long twilight stayed
And, for a whim, that whispered whim obeyed.

There was no breath, no sigh,
No wind lost in the sky
Roamed the horizon round.
The harsh dead leaf slept noiseless on the ground,
By unseen mouse nor insect stirred
Nor beak of hungry bird.

Then were voices heard
Mingling as though each
Earth and grass had individual speech.
—Has evening fallen so soon,
And yet no Moon?
—No, but hark: so still
Was never the Spring's voice adown the hill!
I do not feel her waters tapping upon
The culvert's under stone.
—And if 'tis not yet night a thrush should sing.
—Or if 'tis night the owl should his far echo bring
Near, near.—And I
Should know the hour by his long-shaking distant cry.
—But how should echo be? The air is dead,
No song, no wing,
—No footfall overhead
Of beast,—Or labourer passing, and no sound
Of labourer's Good-night, good-night, good-night!
—That we, here underground,
Take to ourselves and breathe unheard Good-night!
—O, it is lonely now with not one sound
Neath that arched profound,
—No throttled note
Sweet over us to float,
—No shadow treading light
Of man, beast, bird.
—If, earth in dumb earth, lie we here unstirred,
—Why, brother, it were death renewed again
If sun nor rain,
—O death undying, if no dear human touch nor sound
Fall on us underground!

THE CAVES

Like the tide—knocking at the hollowed cliff
And running into each green cave as if

In the cave's night to keep
Eternal motion grave and deep;—

That, even while each broken wave repeats
Its answered knocking and with bruised hand beats
Again, again, again,
Tossed between ecstasy and pain;

Still in the folded hollow darkness swells,
Sinks, swells, and every green-hung hollow fills,
Till there's no room for sound
Save that old anger rolled around;

So into every hollow cliff of life,
Into this heart's deep cave so loud with strife,
In tunnels I knew not,
In lightless labyrinths of thought,

The unresting tide has run and the dark filled,
Even the vibration of old strife is stilled;
The wave returning bears
Muted those time-breathing airs.

—How shall the million-footed tide still tread
These hollows and in each cold void cave spread?
How shall Love here keep
Eternal motion grave and deep?

I WILL ASK

I will ask primrose and violet to spend for you
Their smell and hue,
And the bold, trembling anemone awhile to spare
Her flowers starry fair;
Or the flushed wild apple and yet sweeter thorn
Their sweetness to keep
Longer than any fire-bosomed flower born
Between midnight and midnight deep.

And I will take celandine, nettle and parsley, white
In its own green light,
Or milkwort and sorrel, thyme, harebell and meadowsweet
Lifting at your feet,
And ivy blossom beloved of soft bees; I will take
The loveliest—
The seeding grasses that bend with the winds, and shake

Though the winds are at rest.

"For me?" you will ask. "Yes! surely they wave for you
Their smell and hue,
And you away all that is rare were so much less
By your missed happiness."
Yet I know grass and weed, ivy and apple and thorn
Their whole sweet would keep
Though in Eden no human spirit on a shining morn
Had awaked from sleep.

IN THOSE OLD DAYS

In those old days you were called beautiful,
But I have worn the beauty from your face;
The flowerlike bloom has withered on your cheek
With the harsh years, and the fire in your eyes
Burns darker now and deeper, feeding on
Beauty and the remembrance of things gone.
Even your voice is altered when you speak,
Or is grown mute with old anxiety
For me.

Even as a fire leaps into flame and burns
Leaping and laughing in its lovely flight,
And then under the flame a glowing dome
Deepens slowly into blood-like light:—
So did you flame and in flame take delight,
So are you hollow'd now with aching fire.
But I still warm me and make there my home,
Still beauty and youth burn there invisibly
For me.

Now my lips falling on your silver'd skull,
My fingers in the valleys of your cheeks,
Or my hands in your thin strong hands fast caught,
Your body clutched to mine, mine bent to yours:
Now love undying feeds on love beautiful,
Now, now I am but thought kissing your thought ...
—And can it be in your heart's music speaks
A deeper rhythm hearing mine: can it be
Indeed for me?

THE ASH

The undecaying yew has shed his flowers
Long since in golden showers.
The elm has robed her height
In green, and hangs maternal o'er the bright
Starred meadows, and her full-contented breast
Lifts and sinks to rest.
Shades drowsing in the grass
Beneath the hedge move but as the hours pass.
Beech, oak and beam have all put beauty on
In the eye of the sun.
Because the hawthorn's sweet
All the earth is sweet and the air, and the wind's feet.
In the wood's green hollows the earth is sweet and wet,
For scarce one shaft may get
The sudden green between:
Only that warm sweet creeps between the green;
Or in the clearing the bluebells lifting high
Make another azure sky.

All's leaf and flower except
The sluggish ash that all night long has slept,
And all the morning of this lingering spring.
Every tree else may sing,
Every bough laugh and shake;
But the ash like an old man does not wake
Even though draws near the season's poise and noon
Of heavy-poppied swoon ...
Still the ash is asleep,
Or from his lower upraised palms now creep
First green leaves, promising that even those gaunt
Tossed boughs shall be the haunt
Of Autumn starlings shrill
Mid his full-leaved high branches never still.

If to any tree,
'Tis to the ash that I might likened be—
Masculine, unamenable, delaying,
With palms uplifted praying
For another life and Spring
Yet unforeshadowed; but content to swing
Stiff branches chill and bare
In this fine-quivering air
That others' love makes sweetness everywhere.

To make a fairer,
A kinder, a more constant world than this;
To make time longer
And love a little stronger,

To give to blossoms
And trees and fruits more beauty than they bear,
Adding to sweetness
The aye-wanted completeness,

To say to sorrow,
"Ease now thy bosom of its snaky burden";
(And sorrow brightened,
No more stung and frightened),

To cry to death,
"Stay a little, O proud Shade, thy stony hand";
(And death removing
Left us amazed loving);—

For this and this,
O inward Spirit, arm thyself with power;
Be it thy duty
To give a body to beauty.

Thine to remake
The world in thy hid likeness, and renew
The fading vision
In spite of time's derision.

Be it thine, O spirit,
The world of sense and thought to exalt with light;
Purge away blindness,
Terror and all unkindness.

Shine, shine
From within, on the confused grey world without
That, growing clearer,
Grows spiritual and dearer.

NO MORE ADIEU

Unconscious on thy lap I lay,
A spiritual thing,
Stirless until the yet unlooked-for day

Of human birth
Should call me from thy starry twilight, Earth.
And did thy bosom rock and clear voice sing?
I know not—now no more a spiritual thing.
Nor then thy breathed Adieu
I rightly knew.

—Until those human kind arms caught
And nursed my head
Upon her breast who from the twilight brought
This stranger me.
Mother, it were yet happiness to be
Within your arms; but now that you are dead
Your memory sleeps in mine; so mine is comforted,
Though I breathed dear Adieu
Unheard by you.

And I have gathered to my breast
Wife, mistress, child,
Affections insecure but tenderest
Of all that clutch
Man's heart with their "Too little!" and "Too much!"
O, what anxieties, what passions wild
Bind and unbind me, what storms never to be stilled
Until Adieu, Adieu
Breathe the night through.

O, when all last farewells are said
To these most dear;
O, when within my purged heart peace is shed;
When these old sweet
Humanities move out on hushing feet,
And all is hush; then in that silence clear
Who is it comes again—near and near and near,
Even while the sighed Adieu
Fades the hush through?

O, is it on thy breast I fall,
A spiritual thing
Once more, and hear with ear insensual
The voice of primal Earth
Breathed gently as on Eden faint airs forth;
And so contented to thy bosom cling,
Though all those loves are gone nor faithful echoes ring,
Nor fond Adieu, Adieu
My parted spirit pursue?

—So hidden in green darkness deep,

Feel when I wake
The tides of night and day upon thee sweep,
And know thy forehead bared before the East,
And hear thy forests hushing in the West
And in thy bosom, Earth, the slow heart shake:
But hear no more the infinite forest murmurs break
Into Adieu, Adieu,
No more Adieu!

THE VISIT

I reached the cottage. I knew it from the card
He had given me—the low door heavily barred,
Steep roof, and two yews whispering on guard.

Dusk thickened as I came, but I could smell
First red wallflower and an early hyacinth bell,
And see dim primroses. "O, I can tell,"

I thought, "they love the flowers he loved." The rain
Shook from fruit bushes in new showers again
As I brushed past, and gemmed the window pane.

Bare was the window yet, and the lamp bright.
I saw them sitting there, streamed with the light
That overflowed upon the enclosing night.

"Poor things, I wonder why they've lit up so,"
A voice said, passing on the road below.
"Who are they?" asked another. "Don't you know?"

Their voices crept away. I heard no more
As I crossed the garden and knocked at the door.
I waited, then knocked louder than before,

And thrice, and still in vain. So on the grass
I stepped, and tap-tapped on the rainy glass.
Then did a girl without turning towards me pass

From the room. I heard the heavy barred door creak,
And a voice entreating from the doorway speak,
"Will you come this way?"—a voice childlike and quick.

The way was dark. I followed her white frock,
Past the now-chiming, sweet-tongued unseen clock,
Into the room. One figure like a rock

Draped in an unstarred night—his mother—bowed
Unrising and unspeaking. His aunt stood
And took my hand, murmuring, "So good, so good!"

Never such quiet people had I known.
Voices they scarcely needed, they had grown
To talk less by the word than muted tone.

"We'll soon have tea," the girl said. "Please sit here."
She pushed a heavy low deep-seated chair
I knew at once was his; and I sat there.

I could not look at them. It seemed I made
Noise in that quietness. I was afraid
To look or speak until the aunt's voice said,

"You were his friend." And that "You were!" awoke
My sense, and nervousness found voice and spoke
Of what he had been, until a bullet broke

A too-brief friendship. The rock-like mother kept
Night still around her. The aunt silently wept,
And the girl into the screen's low shadow stept.

"You were great friends," said with calm voice the mother.
I answered, "Never friend had such another."
Then the girl's lips, "Nor sister such a brother."

Her words were like a sounding pebble cast
Into a hollow silence; but at last
She moved and bending to my low chair passed

Swift leaf-like fingers o'er my face and said,
"You are not like him." And as she turned her head
Into full light beneath the lamp's green shade

I saw the sunken spaces of her eyes.
Then her face listening to my dumb surprise.
"Forgive," she said, "a blind girl's liberties."

"You were his friend; I wanted so to see
The friends my brother had. Now let's have tea."
She poured, and passed a cup and cakes to me.

"These are my cakes," she smiled; and as I ate
She talked, and to the others cup and plate
Passed as they in their shadow and silence sat.

"Thanks, we are used to each other," she said when I
Rose in the awkwardness of seeing, shy
Of helping and of watching helplessly.

And from the manner of their hands 'twas clear
They too were blind; but I knew they could hear
My pitiful thoughts as I sat aching there.

... I needs must talk, until the girl was gone
A while out of the room. The lamp shone on,
But the true light out of the room was gone.

"Rose loved him so!" her mother said, and sighed.
"He was our eyes, he was our joy and pride,
And all that's left is but to say he died."

She ceased as Rose returned. Then as before
We talked and paused until, "Tell me once more,
What was it he said?" And I told her once more.

She listened: in her face was pride and pain
As in her mind's eye near he stood and plain....
Then the thin leaves fell on my cheek again

And on my hands. "He must have loved you well,"
She whispered, as her hands from my hands fell.
Silence flowed back with thoughts unspeakable.

It was a painful thing to leave them there
Within the useless light and stirless air.
"Let me show you the way. Mind, there's a stair

"Here, then another stair ten paces on....
Isn't there a moon? Good-bye."
And she was gone.
Full moon upon the drenched fruit garden shone.

TRAVELLING

They talked of old campaigns, nineteen-fourteen
And Mons and watery Yser, nineteen-fifteen
And Neuve Chapelle, 'sixteen, 'seventeen, 'eighteen
And after. And they grumbled, leaving home,
Then talked of nineteen-nineteen, nineteen-twenty
And after.

Their thoughts wandered, leaving home
Among familiar places and known years;
Anticipating in the river, of time
Rocks, rapids, shallows, idle glazing pools
Mirroring their dark dreams of heaven and earth.
—And then they parted, one to Chatham, one
To Africa, Constantinople one,
One to Cologne; and all to an unknown year,
Nineteen-nineteen perhaps, or another year.

THE SONG OF THE FOREST

I

To Thee, Most Holy, Most Obscure, light-hidden,
Shedding light in the darkness of the mind
As gold beams wake the air to birds a-wing;
To Thee, if men were trees, would forests bow
In all our land, as under a new wind;
To Thee, if trees were men, would forests sing
Lifting autumnal crowns and bending low,
Rising and falling again as inly chidden,
Singing and hushing again as inly bidden.
To Thee, Most Holy, men being men upraise
Bright eyes and waving hands of unarticulating praise.

II

To Thee, Most Holy, Most Obscure, who pourest
Thy darkness into each wild-heaving human forest,
While some say, "'Tis so dark God cannot live,"
And some, "It is so dark He never was,"
And few, "I hear the forest branches give
Assurèd signs His wind-like footsteps pass;"
To Thee, now that long darkness is enlightened,
Lift men their hearts, shaking the death-chill dews.
Even sad eyes with morning light are brightened,
And in this spiritual Easter's lovely hues
Are no more with death's arctic shadow frightened.

III

Here in this morning twilight gleaming pure
Mid the high forest boughs and making clear
The motion the night-wakeful brain had guessed;

Here in this peace that wonders, Is it Peace?
And sighs its satisfaction on the shivering air;
Here, O Most Holy, here, O bright Obscure,
Every deep root within the earth's quick breast
Knows that the long night's ended and sore agitations cease,
And every leaf of every human tree
In England's forest stirs and sings, Light Giver, now to Thee.

IV

I cannot syllable that unworded praise—
An ashen sapling bending in Thy wind,
Uplifting in Thy light new-budded leaves;
Nor for myself nor any other raise
My boughs in music, though the woodland heaves—
O with what ease of pain at length resigned,
What hope to the old inheritance restored!
Thy praise it is that men at last are glad.
Long unaccustomed brightness in their eyes
Needs must seem beautiful in thine, bright Lord,
And to forget the part that sorrow had
In every shadowed breast, where still it lies,
Is there not praise in such forgetfulness?
For to grieve less means not that love is less.

V

—Nor for myself nor any other. Yet
I cannot but remember all that passed
Since justice shook these bosoms, and the fret
Of indignation stirred them and they cast
Forgot aside all lesser wrongs, and rose
Against the spiritual evil of that threat
That made them of dishonour slaves or foes.
And who may but with pride remember how
Not by ten righteous justice might be saved,
But by unsaintly millions moving all
As the tide moves when myriad tossed waves flow
One way, and on the crumbling bastions fall;
Then sinking backwards unopposed and slow
Over the ruined towers where those vain angers raved.

VI

Creep tarnished gilded figures to their holes
Who once walked like great men upon the earth
Flickering their false shadows. Fear, like a hound,
Hunts them, and there's a death in every sound;

And had they souls sorrow would prick their souls
At every heavy sigh the wind waved forth.
... Into their holes they've crept, and they will die.
Of them no more and never any more.
Their leper-gilt is gone, and they will lie
Poisoning a little earth and nothing more.

VII

—That justice has been saved and wrong been slain,
That the slow fever-darkness ends in day,
Nor madness shakes the pillared world again
With the same blind proud fury; that in vain
Whispers the Tempter now, "So pass away
Strength, honesty and hope, and nothing left but pain!"
That the many-voiced confusion of the night
Clears in the winging of a spirit bright
With new-recovered joy;—for this, O Light,
Light Giver, Night Dispeller, praise should be.
But praise is dumb from burning hearts to Thee.

VIII

But as a forest bending in the wind
Murmurs in all its boughs after the wind,
Sounds uninterpreted and untaught airs;
So now when Thy wind over England stirs,
The proud and untranslating sounds of praise
Mingle tumultuous over our human ways;
And magnifying echoes of Thy wind
Rouse in the profoundest forests of the mind.

IX

And in the secret thicket where Thy light
Is dimmed with starry shining of the night,
Hearing these mingled airs from every wood
Thou'lt smile serenely down, murmuring, "'Tis good."
While Angels in the thicket borders curled
Amid the farthest gold beams of Thy hair,
Seeing on one drooped beam this distant world
Floating illumined, cry, "Bright Lord, how fair!"

When man first walked upright and soberly
Reflecting as he paced to and fro,
And no more swinging from wide tree to tree,
Or sheltered by vast boles from sheltered foe,
Or crouched within some deep cave by the sea
Stared at the noisy waste of water's woe
Where the earth ended, and far lightning died
Splintered upon the rigid tideless tide;

When man above Time's cloud lifted his head
And speech knew, and the company of speech,
And from his alien presence wild beasts fled
And birds flew wary from his arrow's reach,
And cattle trampling the long meadow weed
Did sentry in the wind's path set; when each
Horn, hoof, claw, sting and sinew against man
Was turned, and the old enmity began;

When, following, beneath the hand of kings
Moved men their parting ways, and some passed on
To forest refuge, some by dark-browed springs,
And some to high remoter pastures won,
And some o'er yellow deserts spread their wings,
Thinning with time and thirst and so were gone
Forgotten; when between each wandered host
The seldom travellers faltered and were lost;—

In those old days, upon the soft dew'd sward
That held its green between the thicket's cloud,
Walked two men musing ere the wide moon poured
Her full-girthed weightless flood. And one was bowed
With years past knowledge, and his face was scored
Where light or deep had every long year ploughed—
Pain, labour, present peril, distant dread
Scored in his brow and bending his shagged head.

Palsy his frame shook as a harsh wind shakes
Complaining reeds fringing a frozen river;
His eye the aspect had of frozen lakes
Whereunder the foiled waters swirl and quiver;
His voice the deep note that the north wind takes
Drawn through bare beechwoods where forlorn birds shiver—
Deep and unfaltering. A younger man
Listened, while warmer currents in him ran.

"Was not my son even as myself to me,
As you to him showed his own life again?
Now he is dead, and all I looked to see

In him removes to you—less near and plain,
Confused with other blood; and what will be
I groping cannot tell, and grope in vain.
For men have turned to other ways than mine:
Yourself are less fulfilment than a sign,

"Sign of a changing world. And change I fear.
I have seen old and young like brief gnats die,
And have faced death by plague and flood and spear:
I have seen mine own familiar people lie
In generations reaped; and near and near
Age leads on Death—I hear his husky sigh.
Yet Death I fear not, but these clouds of change
Sweeping the old firm world with new and strange.

"Son of my son, to whom the world shines new,
You are strange to me for whom the world is old.
Your thoughts are not my thoughts, and unto you
The past, sole warmth for me, is void and cold.
Another passion pours your spirit through,
Another faith has leapt upon the fold
And wrestles with the ancient faith. 'And lo!'
Lightly men say, 'Even the gods come and go!'"

He paused awhile in pacing and hung still,
Amid the thickening shades a darker shade.
Down the steep valley from the barren hill
A herd of deer with antlered leader made
Brief apparition. Mist brimmed up until
Only the great round heights yet solid stayed—
Then they too changed to spectral, and upon
The changing mist wavered, and were gone....

"Standing to-day your father's grave beside,
I knew my heart with his was covered there;
O, more than flesh did in the cold earth hide—
My past, his promise. There was none to care
Save for the body of a prince that died
As princes die; there was none whispered, 'Where
Moves now among us his unburied part?
What breast beats with the pulses of his heart?'

"—Vain thoughts are these that but a dying man
Searches among the dark caves of his mind!
But as I stood, the very wind that ran
Between the files breathed more than common wind,
As though the gods of men when Time began,
Fathers of fathers of old humankind,

Startled, heard now the changeful future knock;
And their lament it was from rock to rock

"Tossed with the wind's long echo ... O, speak not,
Nor tell me with my loss I am so dazed,
That my tongue speaks unfaithfully my thought;
That you, you too, within his shadow raised,
Stand bare now, wanting all you held or thought,
By aimless love or prisoned grief amazed.
Tell me not: let me out of silence speak,
Or let me still my thoughts in silence break."

And so both stood, and not a word to say,
By silence overborne, until at last
The young man breathed, "Look how the end of day
Falls heavily, as though the earth were cast
Into a shapeless soundless pit, where ray
Of heavenly light never the verge has past.
Yet will the late moon's light anon shine here,
And then gray light, and then the sun's light clear.

"Sire, 'twas my father died, and like night's pit
Soundless and shapeless yawn my orphaned years.
And yet I know morn comes and brings with it
Old tasks again, and new joys, hopes and fears.
Or sword or plough these fingers will find fit,
And morrows end with other cries and tears,
With women's arms and children's voices and
The sacred gods blessing the new-sown land.

"But look, upon your beard the dew is bright,
Chill is the winter fall: let us go in."
Then moved they slowly downward till a light
Shining the door-post and thonged door between
Showed the square Prince's House. Out of the night
They passed the sudden rubied warmth within.
Curled shadowy by the wall a servant slept:
A sleepy hound from the same corner crept.

Soon were they couched. The young man fell asleep;
While the old Prince drowsing uneasily,
Tossing on the crest of agitations deep,
Dreamed waking, waking dreamed. Then memory
The unseen hound, did from her corner creep
Into his bosom and stirred him with her sigh
Soundless. And he arose and answering pressed
Her beloved head yet closer to his breast....

Happy those years returned when first he strode
Beside his father's knees, or climbed and felt
The warm strength of those arms, or singing rode
High on his shoulders; or in winter pelt
Of dread beasts wrapt, set as his father showed
Snares in the frosty grass, and at dawn knelt
Beside the snares, and shouting homeward tore,
Winged with such pride as seldom manhood wore.

—How many, many, many years ago!
There was no older man now walked the earth.
Had all those years sunk to a bitter glow,
Like the fire lingering yet upon the hearth?
Ah, he might warm his hands there still, and so
Must warm his heart now in this wintry dearth,
Till the reluming sunken fire should give
Warmth to his ageing wits and bid him live.

Even this house! It was his father told
How in the days half lost in icy time
Men first forsook their wormy caves and cold
To build where the wind-footed cattle climb;
And noise of labour broke the silence old
By such unbroken since the sparkling prime
Of the world's spring. And so the house arose,
A builded cave, perpetual as the snows

On the remotest summits of the range
Hemming the north. Then house by house appeared
'Neath valley-eaves, and change following on change
Unnoted tamed earth's shaggy front. Men heard
Strange voices syllabling with accents strange,
By travellers breathed who, startled, paused and feared
Seeing the smoke of habitations curled
Above this hollow of an unrumoured world.

Startled, they paused and spoke by doubtful sign,
Answered by hesitating sign, until
Moved one with aspect fearless and benign,
And met one fearless, while all else hung still.
And then was welcome, rest, and meat and wine
And intercourse of uncouth word, as shrill
Voice with deep voice was mingled. So they stayed
And to astonished eyes strange arts betrayed.

By them the oarage of the wind was taught,
And how the quick tail steered the cockled boat.
They netted fruitful streams, and smiling brought

Their breaking wickers home, too full to float.
And opening the earth's rich womb they wrought
Arms from the sullied ore; and labouring smote
The mountain's bosom, till a path was seen
Stony amid the flushed snow and flushed green.

Then first upon earth's wave the silver share
Floated, by the teamed oxen drawn; then first
Were seed-time rites, and harvest rites when bare
The cropped fields lay, and gathered tumult—nurst
Long in the breasts of men that laboured there—
Now in the broad ease of fulfilment burst;
And when the winter tasks failed in days chill,
Weaving of bright-hued yarn, and chattering shrill;

And the loved tones of music sounded sweet
Unwonted, when the new-stopped pipe was heard
Rising and falling, and the falling feet
Of sudden dancers. And old men were stirred
With old men's memories of ancient heat
When youth sang in their bosoms like a bird....
Sweet that divine musician, Memory,
Fingering her many-reeded melody.

Then as he stared into the wasting glow
And watched the fire faint in the whitening wood,
Came starker shadows moving vast and slow,
And echoes of wild strife and smell of blood,
Twitching of slain men, cries of parting woe,
Bruised bodies ghastly in the mountain flood;
Burials and burnings, triumph with terrors blent,
And widowed languors and night-long lament.

Like seeds long buried, these dead memories
Upthrust in their new green and spread to flower:
An eager child against his father's knees
Leaning, he had listened many an evening hour.
Now these remote reworded histories
Entangled with his own renewed their power,
Breathing an antique virtue through his mind,
As through dense yew boughs breathes the undying wind.

Sighing, he rose up softly. On the wall
A dark shape shambled aimless to and fro;
Head bent, eyes inward-seeing, rugged, tall,
Himself a shadow moved with musings slow
Amid his cumbered past, and heard sweet call
Of mother voice, and mother folk, and flow

Of gentle and proud speech and tender laughter,
Story and song, fault and forgiveness after;

And a voice graver, gentler than a man
Might hear from any but a woman beloved,
Stilling and awakening the blood that ran
Like ocean tide, as neared she or removed ...
Faded that music. Then a voice began
Paining within his heart, yet unreproved;
For dear the anguish is that steals upon
A father's spirit lamenting his lost son.

—The latest born and latest lost of those
Of his strong and her gentle being born.
By earthquake, pestilence, by human foes
Long were they dead; and yet not all forlorn
He grieved, for at his side the youngest rose
Bright as a willow gilded by dewy morn....
Felled now the tree, silent that music, still
The motion that did all the vale-air fill.

Once more they bore the body from the hunt
Where he alone had died. Once more he heard
The wail and sigh, and saw once more their front
Of drooping grief; once more the wailing stirred
Old hounds to baying wilder than was wont;
Fell once more like slow, sullen rain each word
Reluctant, telling to his senses strayed,
How while the gods drowsed and men hung afraid.

Slain was the Prince unwary by the paw
Of a springing beast that died in giving death.
Again the featureless torn face he saw,
The ribboned bosom emptied of warm breath;
Again the circle sudden hush'd with awe,
And smothered moaning heard the hush beneath.
Again, again, and every night again,
Vision renewed and voice recalled in vain.

Again those dear and lamentable rites
Within the winter stems of forest shade,
The pile, the smokeless flame, the thousand lights,
The one light that in all the thousand played;
Deep burthened voices while, around the heights
Lifting, young trebles their wild echo made;
Then the returning torches at the pyre
Lit, when the eye glowed faint within the fire.

Even as a man that by slow steps may climb
An unknown mountain path with tired tread
By ice-fringed brook and close herb white with rime,
Sees sudden far below a strange land spread
Immense; so from his lonely crag of Time
The Prince, his eye bewildered and adread,
Gazed at the vast, with mist and storm confused,
Cloud-racked, and changing even while he mused.

Ending were the old wise and stable ways.
Adventurers into distant lands had fared,
From distant lands adventurers with gaze
Proud and unenvying on his kingdom stared,
And sojourning had shaken quiet days
With restless knowledge, and strange worship reared
Of foreign altars, idols, prayers and songs
And sacrifice as to such gods belongs.

And all unsatisfied his people grown
Would move from this rejected mountain range
By yearlong valley journeys slowly down,
Sun-following, till surfeited with change,
Mid idle pastures pitched or fabled town,
Subdued to climes and kings and customs strange,
At length their very name should die away
And all their remnant be a vague "Men say."

"Men say!" he sighed, and from that lofty verge
Of inward seeing drooped his doubtful sight.
Sweet was it from such reverie to emerge
And breathe once more the thoughtless air of night,
And watch the fire-slave through fresh billets urge
The sleeping flame, until the vivid light
And toothed shadows wearied.... And then crept
The hounds a little nearer, and all slept.

But the young man still lay in quiet sleep,
Or half-sleep, and a dream-born cloud enwreathed
With memories, hopes and longings hidden deep
In his flown mind. Another air he breathed,
Saw from an unsubstantial mountain sweep
In purest light, soon in low shadow sheathed,
Semblance of faint-known faces, or beloved
Daily-acquainted still, or long removed.

Even as sacred fire in fennel stalks
Through windy ways is borne and densest night,
Till where the outpost shivering sentry walks

Beating the minutes into hours, the light
Touches the guarded pile and, flaring, balks
Beasts padding near and each unvisioned sprite
By old dread apprehended; and new gladness
Shakes in the village prone in winter sadness:—

So through the young man's dream the kingly flame
In his own breast was undiminished borne.
And other peoples catching from his fame
A noble heat, in neighbouring lands forlorn,
Would glow with new power and the ancient name
Bless, that had brightened through their narrow morn.
And purer yet and steadier would pass on
The sacred flame to son and son and son.

Or with contracting mind he saw the host
Of mountain warriors banded, moving down
Untrodden ways, as on young buds a frost
Falls, and the spring lies stiff. The air was sown
With strife, the fields with blood, the night with ghost
Wandering by ghost, and wounded men were strown
Surprised, unweaponed; and chill air congealed
Each hurt, and with the blood their breath was sealed.

And the loved tones of music sounded fierce
When the returning files with aspect proud
Approached, and brandished their rich trophied spears.
Sweet the pipes' spearlike music, sweet and loud,
And music of smitten arms was sweet to tears;
Sweet the dance unto smiling gods new vowed,
Sweet the recounting song and choral cries,
And age's quaverings and girls' envious sighs.

—So of himself, a father-king, he dreamed,
Holding an equal nation in his eye.
O with what golden points the future gleamed!
Rustled the years like laden mule-trains by,
Each with its burthen of old time redeemed....
Splendour on splendour poured, and so would lie
Unnoted and unmeasured:—metals, herds,
Distant-sought wonders, strange growths, beasts and birds.

Within the summer of that splendid shade
Might men live happy and nought left to fear,
Or if an antique restless spirit played
Fretful within their bones, and change drew near
Drumming wild airs, and another music made,
A father-king, speaking assured and clear,

Bidding them follow he would lead them forth
Through the yet undiscovered frowning north.

And the last fire on the warm stones would burn,
And the smoke linger on the mountain skies.
And seeing, they would muse yet of return
And then forget their sadness in the cries
Confused of the great caravan; and so turn
Towards the next sun-setting and the next sunrise
Many and many a day and wind and wind
Through foreign earth, as a dream through the mind.

Flowing on with the changes of its thought.
And doubtful kings entreating them to stay
Would sleep the easier when they lingered not;
And sullen tribes menacing would make way,
And broad slow rivers in their tide be caught,
And the long caravan o'er the ford all day
And all day and all day pass; while the tide slept
In sluggish shallows, or through marsh-reeds crept.

So would they on and on, with death and birth
For wayfellows and nightly stars for guide,
While seasons bloomed and faded on the earth,
And jealous gods their wandering gods would chide.
Until, weary of endless going forth
Dark-locust-like, the old fret would subside,
And young men with aged men and women cry,
"In this full-rivered pasture let us lie!

"Here let us lie, and wanderings be at rest!"
Midmost a cedar grove high sacrifice
Needs then be made, that gods be manifest;
And while the smoke spread in long twilit skies,
"Here let us lie, and wanderings be at rest,"
Would old men breathe repeated between sighs.
"In this green world and cool," would mothers say,
"Rest we, nor with thin babes yet longer stray."

—So stealing from the mind of the old King
Exhausted, into the sleeping young man's brain
Crept the same dream and lifted on new wing
And took from his swift passions a new stain,
Sanguine and azure, and first fluttering
Rose then on easy vans that bore again
The sleeper past his common thought's confine:—
So borne, so soaring, in that air divine,

He saw his people stayed, their journeys ended....
There should they, no more fretful, dwell for ever
In the full-nourished pasture where untended
Herds multiplied, and famine threatened never,
And where high border-hills glittered with splendid
Sparse-covered veins washed by the hill-born river.
So stead by stead arose, and men there moved
Satisfied, and no more vain longings roved.

Again the silver plough gleamed in the sod,
And seed from old fields slept in furrows new.
Then when Spring's rain and sun together trod
And interweaved swift steps the meadow through,
Old rites revived; they bore the shapen god
With green stalks and first-budded boughs, and drew
Together youth and age. And sowers leapt
High o'er the seed in earth's cold bosom wrapt:—

So in the golden-hued and burning hours
Of harvest, leapt on high the full-eared corn.
Friendly to pious hands those imaged Powers
Of rain and sun. And when the grain was borne
By oxen trailing tangled straws and flowers,
With leaves and dying blossoms on each horn,
Friendly the gods commingling in the shades
Of moon and torch and smoke-delaying glades.

Fell slowly sunset; the starred evening cool
Drooped round as mid his people the king rode,
Blessing and blessed, and in the faithful pool
Of their old loves his clear reflection glowed
Like summer's golden moon:—in wise and fool,
Noble and mean, accustomed reverence showed
Clear-shining; so he reached the unbarred hall
Where lamps, lords, servitors flashed festival,

Remembering old journeys and their end.
Bright-throned he sat there, with those lords around
Snow-polled, co-eval, as with friends their friend
Feasting. Arose at length the awaited sound
Of bardic chanting, bidding their thoughts descend
Into the chamber where the Past lay bound,
Wanting but music's finger; so upspringing,
The Past stormed all their minds in that loud singing.

And strangers, furred and tawny, seated there,
Far travellers from the sunrise, looking on
The feasting and the splendour, and with ear

Uncertain listening to the solemn tone
Of most dear Memory, envied all and sware
A sudden fealty. But the bard sang on
While silver beakers brimmed untouched; and darkened
The proud remembering eyes of men that hearkened.

Then came once more those strangers leading long
Migration of their subject folk. They stayed
And medley'd and were mingled, and their throng
Melted in his like snows, and so were made
One with them, and forgot their useless tongue,
Nor now their ancient bloody worship paid
To painted gods:—name, language, story died
When their last faithless exile parting sighed.

So year on year, century on century
In his imagination of delight
Followed, in a new world all innocency
And simpleness, and made for beings bright,
Where man to man was friend, unfearful, free,
And natural griefs alone darkened their night,
And natural joys as the wide air were common,
And kindness was the bond of all kin human.

—When the loved reeds of music sounded clear
From birds' breasts quivering in tall woodland trees
That rustled leafless in the winter air,
And with morn's new voice shrilled the western breeze:
Folding her wings the dream crept from his ear
To hang where bats drowse until daylight dies.
Then he from sleep's dear vanity awaking
Watched a sole sunbeam the roof-shadows raking.

PART II

THE WAKERS

The joyous morning ran and kissed the grass
And drew his fingers through her sleeping hair,
And cried, "Before thy flowers are well awake
Rise, and the lingering darkness from thee shake.

"Before the daisy and the sorrel buy
Their brightness back from that close-folding night,
Come, and the shadows from thy bosom shake,
Awake from thy thick sleep, awake, awake!"

Then the grass of that mounded meadow stirred
Above the Roman bones that may not stir
Though joyous morning whispered, shouted, sang:
The grass stirred as that happy music rang.

O, what a wondrous rustling everywhere!
The steady shadows shook and thinned and died,
The shining grass flashed brightness back for brightness,
And sleep was gone, and there was heavenly lightness.

As if she had found wings, light as the wind,
The grass flew, bent with the wind, from east to west,
Chased by one wild grey cloud, and flashing all
Her dews for happiness to hear morning call....

But even as I stepped out the brightness dimmed,
I saw the fading edge of all delight.
The sober morning waked the drowsy herds,
And there was the old scolding of the birds.

MEMORIES OF CHILDHOOD TO MARJORY

I

CHILDHOOD CALLS

Come over, come over the deepening river,
Come over again the dark torrent of years,
Come over, come back where the green leaves quiver,
And the lilac still blooms and the grey sky clears.

Come, come back to the everlasting garden,
To that green heaven, and the blue heaven above.
Come back to the time when time brought no burden
And love was unconscious, knowing not love.

II

THE ANSWER

O, my feet have worn a track
Deep and old in going back.
Thought released turns to its home

As bees through tangling thickets come.
One way of thought leads to the vast
Desert of the mind, and there is lost,
But backward leads to a dancing light
And myself there, stiff with delight.
O, well my thought has trodden a way
From this brief day to that long day.

III

THE FIRST HOUSE

That is the earliest thing that I remember—
The narrow house in the long narrow street,
Dark rooms within and darkness out of doors
Where grasses in the garden lift in the wind,
Long grasses clinging round unsteady feet.
The sunlight through one narrow passage pours,
As through the keyhole into a dusty room,
Striking with a golden rod the greening gloom.
The tall, tall timber-stacks have yet been kind,
Letting the sun fling his rod clear between,
Lest there should be no gold upon the green,
And no light then for a child to dream upon,
And day be of day's brightness all forlorn.
I saw those timber piles first dark and tall,
And then men clambered up, and stumbled down,
Each with a heavy and long timber borne
Upon broad shoulders, leather-covered, bent.
Hour after hour, day after day they went,
Until the piles were gone and a new sky
Stretched high and white above the garden wall.
And then fresh piles crept slowly up and up,
The strong men staggering, more cruelly bowed,
Till at last they lay idle on the top
Looking down from their height on things so small,
While I looked wondering and fearful up
At the strong men at rest on the new-built cloud.
But there was other gold than the sun's sparse gold—
Florence's hair, its brightness lying still
Upon my mind as then upon the grass.
Now the grass covers it and I am old,
Remembering but her hair and that long grass,
And the great wood-stacks threatening to fall—
When all dark things will.

THE OTHER HOUSE

That other house, in the same crowded street,
One red-tiled floor had, answering to my feet,
And a bewildering garden all of light and heat.

Only that red floor and garden now remain,
One glowing firelike in my glowing brain,
One with smell, colour, sun and cloud revived again.

Yet in the garden the sky was very small,
Closed by some darkness beyond the low brown wall;
But from the west the gold could long unhindered fall.

Of human faces I remember none
Amid the garden; but myself alone
With creeping-jenny, sunflower, marigold, snapdragon—

These all my love, these now all my light,
Bringing their kindness to any painful night.
The sun brushed all their brightness with his skirt more bright.

And I was happy when I knew it not,
Dreaming of nothing more than that small plot,
And the high sky and sun that floated bright and hot.

But what night was, save dark, I did not know.
The blind shut out the stars: the moon would go
Staring, unstared at, moon and stars unnoted flow.

Until one night, into the strange street led,
To stare at a strange light from the Factory shed,
Wheeling and darting, withdrawn, and sudden again outsped—

No one knew why—but I knew darkness then,
And saw the stars that hung so still; but when
I lay abed the old starless dark came back again.

Night is not night without the stars and moon.
I knew them not, or I forgot too soon,
And now remember only the glowing sun of noon,

The red floor, and yellow flowers, and a lonely child,
And a whistle morn and noon and evening shrilled,

And darkness when the household murmurs even were stilled.

V

Near the house flowed, or paused, the black Canal,
Edged by the timber piles so black and tall.
From the rotten fence I watched the horses pull
Along the footpath, slow and beautiful,
Moving with strength and ease, in their great size
And untired movement wonderful to my eyes;
Their dull brass clanking as each shaggy foot
Stamped the soft cinder track as fine as soot.
The driver lurched old and forbidding by,
Not seeing the child that feared to meet his eye.
I watched the rope dip, tighten, and the water flash
In falling, and then heard the hiss and splash;
I watched the barge drag slowly on and on,
Not dreaming how lovely a ship could ride the water upon,
Not dreaming how lovely flowing water was,
Sung to by trees and fingered by long grass,
Or running from the bosom of a hill
Down, where it flows so deep that it seems still.
But it was by that rotten fence one night
I saw the timber piles break into light,
Suddenly leaping into a heavenly flame
That played with the wind and one with the wind became.
Pile to pile gave its fire, till they were like
Bright angels with flashing swords before they strike,
Terrible and lovely. But men those angels fought,
Small and humble and patient all night wrought,
And all day wrought and night and day again,
And night and day, pouring their hissing rain,
Until the angels tired and one by one died.
Then their black spectres haunted the waterside,
Charred ruins, broken-limbed, no more erect,
Or heaped black dust, with cold white ashes flecked.
But I had seen the angel-quelling men,
With blackened and bruised face, the horses thin,
The glittering harness, the leaky, bubbling mains,
The broad smoke, and the steam from the leaping rains:—
O I had seen what I should not forget,
Men that defeated ruinous angels and shall still defeat.

VI

THE KITE

It was a day
All blue and lifting white,
When I went into the fields with Frank
To fly his kite.

The fields were aged, bare,
Shut between houses everywhere.
All the way there
The wind tugged at the kite to take it
Untethered, toss and break it;
But Frank held fast, and I
Walked with him admiringly;
In his light brave and fine
How bright was mine!

We tailed the kite
While the wind flapped its purple face
And yellow head.
Frank's yellow head
Was scarcely higher, and not so bright.
"Let go!" he cried, and I let go
And watched the kite
Swaying and rising so
That I was rooted to the place,
Watching the kite
Rise into the blue,
Lifting its head against the white
Against the sun,
Against the height
That far-off, farther drew;
Shivering there
In that fine air
As we below shivered with delight
And fear.

There it floated
Among the birds and clouds at ease
Of others all unnoted,
Swimming above the ranked stiff trees.
And I lay down, looking up at the sky,
The clouds and birds that floated
By others still unnoted,
And that swaying kite

Specking the light:
Looking up at the sky,
The birds and clouds that drew
Nearer, leaving the blue,
Stooping, and then brushing me,
With such tenderness touching me
That I had still lain there
In those fields bare,
Forgetting the kite;
For every cloud was now a kite
Streaming with light.

VII

THE CHAIR

The chair was made
By hands long dead,
Polished by many bodies sitting there,
Until the wood-lines flowed as clean as waves.

Mine sat restless there,
Or propped to stare
Hugged the low kitchen with fond eyes
Or tired eyes that looked at nothing at all.

Or watched from the smoke rise
The flame's snake-eyes,
Up the black-bearded chimney leap;
Then on my shoulder my dull head would drop.

And half asleep
I heard her creep—
Her never-singing lips shut fast,
Fearing to wake me by a careless breath.

Then, at last,
My lids upcast,
Our eyes met, I smiled and she smiled,
And I shut mine again and truly slept.

Was I that child
Fretful, sick, wild?
Was that you moving soft and soft
Between the rooms if I but played at sleep?

Or if I laughed,
Talked, cried, or coughed,
You smiled too, just perceptibly,
Or your large kind brown eyes said, O poor boy!

From the fireside I
Could see the narrow sky
Through the barred heavy window panes,
Could hear the sparrows quarrelling round the lilac;

And hear the heavy rains
Choking in the roof-drains:—
Else of the world I nothing heard
Or nothing remember now. But most I loved

To watch when you stirred
Busily like a bird
At household doings; with hands floured
Mixing a magic with your cakes and tarts.

O into me, sick, froward,
Yourself you poured;
In all those days and weeks when I
Sat, slept, woke, whimpered, wondered and slept again.

Now but a memory
To bless and harry me
Remains of you still swathed with care;
Myself your chief care, sitting by the hearth

Propped in the pillowed chair,
Following you with tired stare,
And my hand following the wood lines
By dead hands smoothed and followed many years.

VIII

THE SWING

It was like floating in a blessed dream to roam
Across green meadows, far from home,
With only trees and quivering sky to hedge the sight,
Dazzling the eyes with strange delight.
Such wide, wide fields I had never seen, and never dreamed
Could be; and wonderful it seemed
To wander over green and under green and run

Unwatched even of the shining sun.

One tree there was that held a wrinkled creaking bough
Far over the grass, hanging low;
And a swing from it hanging drew us near and made
New brightness beneath that doming shade.
For there my sisters swung long hours delightedly,
And there delighted clambered I;
And all our voices shrilled as one when up we flung
And into the stinging sharp leaves swung.

Then in a garden dense with bramble and sweet flowers
Where honeysuckle a new sweetness pours,
We sat and ate and drank. Well I remember how
We were all shaded by one bough
Bending with red fruit over our uplifted eyes,
Teasing our well-watched covetousness.

And then we went back happy to the empty swing,
But I was tired of everything
Except the grass and trees and the wide shadows there
Widening slowly everywhere.
It was like swinging in a solemn dream to roam
In a strange air, far from home—
Until I saw the shadows suddenly wake and move,
And float, float down from above.
Then I ran quickly back, round the large gloomy trees,
O with what shivering unease!
And stumbled where they waited, and was far too glad,
Finding them, to be afraid or sad.
—Then waited an unforgetting year once more to see
So wide a sky, so great a tree.

IX

FEAR

Surely I must have ailed
On that dark night,
Or my childish courage failed
Because there was no light;
Or terror must have come
With his chill wing,
And made my angel dumb,
Or found him slumbering.
Because I could not sleep

Terror began to wake,
Close at my side to creep
And sting me like a snake.
And I was afraid of death,
But when I thought of pain—
O, language no word hath
To recall that thought again!
Into my heart fear crawled
And wreathed close around,
Mortal, convulsive, cold,
And I lay bound.
Fear set before my eyes
Unimaginable pain;
Approaching agonies
Sprang nimbly into my brain.
Just as a thrilling wind
Plucks every mournful wire,
So terror on my wild mind
Fingered, with ice and fire.
O, not death I feared,
But the anguish of the body;
My dizzying passions heard,
Saw my own bosom bloody.
I thought of years of woe,
Moments prolonged to years,
Heard my heart racing so,
Redoubling all those fears.
Yet still I could not cry,
Not a sound the stillness broke;
But the dark stirred, and my
Negligent angel woke.

X

THE STREETS

Marlboro' and Waterloo and Trafalgar,
Tuileries, Talavera, Valenciennes,
Were strange names all, and all familiar;

For down their streets I went, early and late
(Is there a street where I have never been
Of all those hundreds, narrow, skyless, straight?)—

Early and late, they were my woods and meadows;
The rain upon their dust my summer smell;

Their scant herb and brown sparrows and harsh shadows

Were all my spring. Was there another spring?
I knew their noisy desolation well,
Drinking it up as a child drinks everything,

Knowing no other world than brick and stone,
With one rich memory of the earth all bright.
Now all is fallen into oblivion—

All that I was, in years of school and play,
Things that I hated, things that were delight,
Are all forgotten, or shut all away

Behind a creaking door that opens slow.
But there's a child that walks those streets of war,
Hearing his running footsteps as they go

Echoed from house to house, and wondering
At Marlboro', Waterloo and Trafalgar;
And at night, when the yellow gas lamps fling

Unsteady shadows, singing for company;
Yet loving the lighted dark, and any star
Caught by sharp roofs in a narrow net of sky.

XI

WHEN CHILDHOOD DIED

I can recall the day
When childhood died.
I had grown thin and tall
And eager-eyed.

Such a false happiness
Had seized me then;
A child, I saw myself
Man among men.

Now I see that I was
Ignorant, surprised,
As one for the surgeon's knife
Anæsthetized.

So that I did not know

What loomed before,
Nor how, a child, I became
A child no more.

The world's sharpened knife
Cut round my heart;
Then something was taken
And flung apart.

I did not, could not know
What had been done.
Under some evil drag
I lived as one

At home in the seeming world;
Then slowly came
Through years and years to myself
And was no more the same.

I know now an ill thing was done
To a young child
By the world's wary knife
Maimed and defiled.

I can recall the day
Almost without anger or pain,
When childhood did not die
But was slain.

XII

ALL THAT I WAS I AM

Hateful it seems now, yet was I not happy?
Starved of the things I loved, I did not know
I loved them, and was happy lacking them.
If bitterness comes now (and that is hell)
It is when I forget that I was happy,
Accusing Fate, that sits and nods and laughs,
Because I was not born a bird or tree.
Let accusation sleep, lest God's own finger
Point angry from the cloud in which He hides.
Who may regret what was, since it has made
Himself himself? All that I was I am,
And the old childish joy now lives in me
At sight of a green field or a green tree.

THE SHOCK

Thinking of these, of beautiful brief things,
Of things that are of sense and spirit made,
Of meadow flowers, dense hedges and dark bushes
With roses trailing over nests of thrushes;

Of dews so pure and bright and flush'd and cool,
And like the flowers as brief as beautiful;
Thinking of the tall grass and daisies tall
And whispered music of the waving bents;

Of these that like a simple child I love
Since they are life and life is flowers and grass;
Thinking of trees, and water at their feet
Answering the trees with murmur childlike sweet;

Thinking of those high thoughts that passed like the wind
Yet left their brightness lying on the mind,
As the white blossoms the raw airs shake down
That lie awhile yet lovely on the chill grass;

Thinking of the dark, where all these end like cloud,
And the stars watch like Knights to Honour vowed,
Of those too lovely colours of the East,
And the too tender loveliness of grey:

Thinking of all, I was as one that stands
'Neath the bewildering shock of breaking seas;
Mortal-immortal things had lost their power,
I knew no more than sweetness in the flower;

No more than colour in the changing light,
No more than order in the stars of night;
A breathing tree was but gaunt wood and leaves;
All these had lost their old power over me.

I had forgotten that ever such things were:
Immortal-mortal, I had been but blind ...
O the wild sweetness of the renewing sense
That swept me and drove all but sweetness hence!

... As beautiful as brief—ah! lovelier,
Being but mortal. Yet I had great fear—
That I should die ere these sweet things were dead,

Or live on knowing the wild sweetness fled.

THE UNLOOSENING

Winter was weary. All his snows were failing—
Still from his stiff grey head he shook the rime
Upon the grasses, bushes and broad hedges,
But all was lost in the new touch of Time.

And the bright-globèd hedges were all ruddy,
As though warm sunset glowed perpetual.
The myriad swinging tassels of first hazel,
From purple to pale gold, were swinging all

In the soft wind, no more afraid of Winter.
Nor chaffinch, wren, nor lark was now afraid.
And Winter heard, or (ears too hard of hearing)
Snuffed the South-West that in his cold hair played.

And his hands trembled. Then with voice a-quaver
He called the East Wind, and the black East ran,
Roofing the sky with iron, and in the darkness
Winter crept out and chilled the earth again.

And while men slept the still pools were frozen,
Mosses were white, with ice the long grasses bowed;
The hawthorn buds and the greening honeysuckle
Froze, and the birds were dumb under that cloud.

And men and beasts were dulled, and children even
Less merry, under that low iron dome.
Early the patient rooks and starlings gathered;
Any warm narrow place for men was home.

And Winter laughed, but the third night grew weary,
And slept all heavy, till the East Wind thought him dead.
Then the returning South West in his nostrils
Breathed, and his snows melted. And his head

Uplifting, he saw all the laughing valley,
Heard the unloosened waters leaping down
Broadening over the meadows; saw the sun running
From hill to hill and glittering upon the town.

All day he stared. But his head drooped at evening,
Bent and slow he stumbled into the white

Cavern of a great chalk hill, hedged with tall bushes,
And in its darkness found a darker night

Among the broken cliff and falling water,
Freezing or falling quietly everywhere;
Locked in a long, long sleep, his brain undreaming,
With only water moving anywhere.

Old men at night dreamed that they saw him going,
And looked, and dared not look, lest he should turn.
And young men felt the air beating on their bodies,
And the young women woke from dreams that burn.

And children going through the fields at morning
Saw the unloosened waters leaping down,
And broke the hazel boughs and wore the tassels
Above their eyes—a pale and shaking crown.

WILD HEART

I

DARK AND STRANGE

When first Love came, then was I but a boy
Swept with delirium of undreamt joy.
Now Love comes to a man serious with change
Of life and death—and makes the world dark and strange.

II

WILD HEART

Wild heart, wild heart,
Where does the wind find home?
Wild heart, wild heart,
Where does the wild blood rest?
Home, home,
Rest, rest—
Unto you I come
And catch you to my breast.

Wild heart, wild heart,
There the wind will sleep.

Wild heart, wild heart,
And the blood gently flow.
Come, come,
Unresting rest
Within my heart's cave deep
Where thoughts like bright stars glow.

Wild heart, wild heart,
Here, here is your home.
Wild heart, wild heart,
With that winged star I come.
Home, home,
Rest in unrest—
Unto you, wild heart, I come.
My wild heart is your home.

III

HOME FOR LOVE

Because the earth is vast and dark
And wet and cold;
Because man's heart wants warmth and light
Lest it grow old;

Therefore the house was built—wall, roof
And brick and beam,
By a lost hand following the lost
Delight of a dream,

And room and stair show how that hand
Groped in eager doubt,
With needless weight of teasing timber
Matching his thought—

Such fond superfluousness of strength
In wall and wood
As his half-wise, half-fearful eye
Deemed only good.

His brain he built into the house,
Laboured his bones;
He burnt his heart into the brick
And red hearth-stones.

It is his blood that makes the house
Still warm, safe, bright,

Honest as aim and eye and hand,
As clean, as light.

Because the earth is vast and dark
The house was built—
Now with another heart and fire
To be fulfilled.

IV

THE ALDE

How near I walked to Love,
How long, I cannot tell.
I was like the Alde that flows
Quietly through green level lands,
So quietly, it knows
Their shape, their greenness and their shadows well;
And then undreamingly for miles it goes
And silently, beside the sea.

Seamews circle over,
The winter wildfowl wings,
Long and green the grasses wave
Between the river and the sea.
The sea's cry, wild or grave,
From, bank to low bank of the river rings;
But the uncertain river though it crave
The sea, knows not the sea.

Was that indeed salt wind?
Came that noise from falling
Wild waters on a stony shore?
Oh, what is this new troubling tide
Of eager waves that pour
Around and over, leaping, parting, recalling?...
How near I moved (as day to same day wore)
And silently, beside the sea!

V

AGAINST THE COLD PALE SKY

Against the cold pale sky
The elm tree company rose high.
All the fine hues of day

That flowered so bold had died away.
Only chill blue, faint green,
And deepening dark blue were seen.

There swinging on a bough
That hung or floated broad and low.
The lamp of evening, bright
With more than planetary light,
Was beautiful and free—
A white bird swaying on the tree.

You watched and I watched,
Our eyes and hearts so surely matched.
We saw the white bird leap, leap
Shining in his journey steep
Through that vast cold sky.
Our hearts knew his unuttered cry—

A cry of free delight
Spreading over the clustering night.
Pole Hill grave and stark
Stared at the valley's tidal dark,
The Darent glimmered wan;
But that eager planet winging on,

And singing on, went high
Into the deeps and heights of sky.
And our thoughts rising too
Brightened the mortal darkness through
Trembled and danced and sang
Till the mute invisible heavens rang.

VI

THE DARK FIRE

Love me not less
Yet ease me of this fever,
That in my wondering heart
Burns, sinks, burns again ever.

Is it your love
In me so fiercely burning,
Or my love leaping to you
Then requickened returning?

Come not to me,

Bring not your body nearer,
Though you overleapt the miles
I could not behold you clearer.

I could not clasp you
Than in my thought more surely;
Breast to breast, heart to heart
Might cling no more securely.

I do not know you,
Seeing you, more than unseeing.
What you are that you are
Here in my spiritual being.

Leave me you cannot,
Nor can I remove me
From the sevenfold dark fire
You have lit here since you love me.

Yet love unsure
No wilder could be burning.
Come, go, come, go,
There's neither leaving nor returning.

Love me, love me more.
O, not my heart shall quaver
If the dark fire more deep
Sinks and is sevenfold sevenfold graver.

VII

THE KESTREL

In a great western wind we climbed the hill
And saw the clouds run up, ride high and sink;
And there were shadows running at our feet
Till it seemed the very earth could not be still,
Nor could our hearts be still, nor could we think
Our hearts could ever be still, our thought less fleet
Than the dizzy clouds, less than the flying wind.
Eastward the valley and the dark steep hill
And other hills and valleys lost behind
In mist and light. The hedges were not yet bare
Though the wind picked at them as he went by.
The woods were fire, a fire that dense or clear
Burned steady, but could not burn up the shadows
Rooted where the trees' roots entangled lie,

In darkness; or a flame burned solitary
In the middle of the highest of brown meadows,
Burned solitary and unconsuming where
A red tree stooped to its black shadow and
The kestrel's shadow hunted the kestrel up the hill.
We climbed, and as we stood (where yet we stand
And of the visioned sun and shadow still drink)
Happiness like a shadow chased our thought
That tossed on free wings up and down the world;
Till by that wild swift-darting shadow caught
Our free spirits their free pinions furled.
Then as the kestrel began once more the heavens to climb
A new-winged spirit rose clear above the hills of time.

VIII

THE IMAGE

I am a river flowing round your hill,
Holding your image in my lingering water,
With imaged white clouds rising round your head;
And I am happy to bear your image still.
Though a loud ruffling wind may break and scatter
That happiness, I know it is not fled.

But when the wind is gone or gentled so
That only the least quivering quivers on,
Your image recomposes in my breast
With those high clouds, quiet and white as snow—
Spiritual company; and when day's gone
And those white clouds have stepped into the west;

And the dark blue filling the heavens deep
Is bright with stars that sing above your head,
Their light lies in the deep of my dark eyes
With your dark shape, a shadow of your sleep ...
I am happy still, watching the bright stars tread
Around your shadow that in my bosom lies.

IX

PERVERSITIES

I

Now come,

And I that moment will forget you.
Sit here
And in your eyes I shall not see you.
Speak, speak
That I no more may hear your music.
Into my arms,
Till I've forgotten I ever met you.

I shall not have you when I hold you
Body to body,
Though your firm flesh, though your strong fingers
Be knit to these.
On a wild hill I shall be chasing
The thought of you;
False will be those true things I told you:
I shall forget you.

No, do not come.
Where the wind hunts, there shall I find you.
In cool gray cloud
Where the sun slips through I shall see you,
Or where the trees
Are silenced, and darken in their branches.
Your coming would
Loosen, when my thought still would bind you.

Against my shoulder your warm shoulder
When last you leaned—
Think, were you nearer then and dearer,
Or I more glad?
O eternal love, your body brings you
No nearer.
Trust me, be bold, be even a little bolder
And do not come.

X

PERVERSITIES

II

Yet when I am alone my eyes say, Come.
My hands cannot be still.
In that first moment all my senses ache,
Cells, that were empty fill,
The clay walls shake,
And unimprisoned thought runs where it will.

Runs and is glad and listens and doubts, and glooms
Because you are not here.
Then once more rises and is clear again
As sense is never clear,
And happy, though in vain
These eyes wait and these arms to bring you near.

Yet spite of thought my arms and eyes say, Come,
Pained with such discontent.
For though thought have you all my senses ache—
O, it was not meant
My body should never wake
But on thought's tranquil bosom rest content.

XI

THE VALLEY

Between the beechen hill and the green down
The valley pastures sink;
And the green river runs through their warm green
Northward into the sea.

Dark is the beechen hill these winter days,
The trees swallow the light
And make an evening there when morning shines
And the down heaves to the south.

Only when the sun's low a fire creeps through
The dark of the beechen hill;
While the green down, misty from head to foot,
Grows huge and dim with sleep.

Then in the valley by the yet shining river,
Under the noisy elms,
I know how like twin shadows over me
Rising high, east and west,

Are Love's dark hills, quiet, unchanging, vast,
Sleeping beneath the stars;
While I with those stars in my bosom shining
Move northward to the sea.

XII

THE DARK NIGHT OF THE MIND

I could not love if my thought loved not too,
Nor could my body touch the body of you,
Unless first in the dark night of the mind
Love had fulfilled what Love had well designed.

Was it in thought or flesh we walked, when low
The sun dropped, and the white scar on the hill
Sank into the dark trees?
Could we indeed so quietly go
Body by body into that heavenly glow?

The elms that rose so vast above the mill
Near leafless were and still;
But from the branches with such loud unease
Black flocking starlings mixed their warring cries
That seemed the greater noise of the creaking mill;
And every branch and extreme twig was black
With birds that whistled and heard and whistled back,
Filling with noise as late with wings the skies.
Was it their noise we heard,
Or clamour of other thoughts in our quiet mind that stirred?

Then through the climbing hazel hedge new thinned
By the early and rapacious wind,
We saw the silver birches gleam with light
Of frozen masts in seas all wild and green.
O, were they truly trees, or some unseen
Thought taking on an image dark and bright?
And did those bodies see them, or the mind?
And did those bodies face once more the hill
To bathe in night, or on a darker road
Our spirits unseeing unwearying rise and rise
Where these feet never trod?

From that familiar outer darkness I
Would rise to the inner, deeper, darker sky
And find you in my spirit—or find you not,
O, never, never, if not in my thought.

THE BODY

When I had dreamed and dreamed what woman's beauty was,
And how that beauty seen from unseen surely flowed,
I turned and dreamed again, but sleeping now no more:

My eyes shut and my mind with inward vision glowed.

"I did not think!" I cried, seeing that wavering shape
That steadied and then wavered, as a cherry bough in June
Lifts and falls in the wind—each fruit a fruit of light;
And then she stood as clear as an unclouded moon.

As clear and still she stood, moonlike remotely near;
I saw and heard her breathe, I years and years away.
Her light streamed through the years, I saw her clear and still,
Shape and spirit together mingling night with day.

Water falling, falling with the curve of time
Over green-hued rock, then plunging to its pool
Far, far below, a falling spear of light;
Water falling golden from the sun but moonlike cool:

Water has the curve of her shoulder and breast,
Water falls as straight as her body rose,
Water her brightness has from neck to still feet,
Water crystal-cold as her cold body flows.

But not water has the colour I saw when I dreamed,
Nor water such strength has. I joyed to behold
How the blood lit her body with lamps of fire
And made the flesh glow that like water gleamed cold.

A flame in her arms and in each finger flame,
And flame in her bosom, flame above, below,
The curve of climbing flame in her waist and her thighs;
From foot to head did flame into red flame flow.

I knew how beauty seen from unseen must rise,
How the body's joy for more than body's use was made.
I knew then how the body is the body of the mind,
And how the mind's own fire beneath the cool skin played.

O shape that once to have seen is to see evermore,
Falling stream that falls to the deeps of the mind,
Fire that once lit burns while aught burns in the world,
Foot to head a flame moving in the spirit's wind!

If these eyes could see what these eyes have not seen—
The inward vision clear—how should I look for joy,
Knowing that beauty's self rose visible in the world
Over age that darkens, and griefs that destroy?

They were like dreams that in a drowsy hour
A sad old God had dreamed in loneliness of power.
They were like dreams that in his drowsy mind
Rose slowly and then, darkening, made him wise and blind—
So that he saw no more the level sun,
Nor the small solid shadow of unclouded noon.
The dark green heights rose slowly from the green
Of the dark water till the sky was narrowly seen;
Only at night the lifting walls were still,
And stars were bright and calm above each calm dark hill.
... I could not think but that a God grown old
Saw in a dream or waking all this round of bold
And wavelike hills, and knew them but a thought,
Or but a wave uptost and poised awhile then caught
Back to the sea with waves a million more
That rise and pause and break at last upon the shore.
A God, a God saw first those hills that I
Saw now immense upholding the starry crowded sky:
His breath the mist that clung their shoulders round,
His slow unconscious sigh that easeless floating sound.
Ere mine his thought failed under each rough height
And then was brave, seeing the stars climb calm and bright.
Ere they were named he named them in his mood,
Like varying children of one giant warring brood—
Broad-Foot, Cloud-Gatherer, Long-Back, Winter-Head,
Bravery and Bright-Face and that long Home of the Dead;
And their still waters glittering in his glance
Named Buckler, Silver Dish, Two Eyes and Shining Lance,
Names unrecorded, but the circling wind
Remembers and repeats them to the listening mind....
That mind was mine. At Shining Lance I stared
Between Long-Back and Winter-Head as the new sun bared
The Lake and heights of shadow and the wan gold
Deepened and new warmth came into the light's sharp cold.
And the near trees shivered no more but shook
Their music over Shining Lance; and the excited brook
Freshened in the sun's eye and tossed his spray
High and sparkling, and then sprang dancing, dancing away.
But Winter-Head and Long-Back, gravely bright,
Stood firm as if for ever and a day and a night—
As they were more than a wave before 'tis caught
Back to the tossing tide, more than a flying thought,
More than a dream that an old God once dreamed
When visionary not at all visionary seemed.

THE POND

Gray were the rushes
Beside the budless bushes,
Green-patched the pond.
The lark had left soaring
Though yet the sun was pouring
His gold here and beyond.

Bramble-branches held me,
But had they not compelled me
Yet had I lingered there
Hearing the frogs and then
Watching the water-hen
That stared back at my stare.

There amid the bushes
Were blackbird's nests and thrush's,
Soon to be hidden
In leaves on green leaves thickening,
Boughs over long boughs quickening
Swiftly, unforbidden.

The lark had left singing
But song all round was ringing,
As though the rushes
Were sighingly repeating
And mingling that most sweet thing
With the sweet note of thrushes.

That sweetness rose all round me,
But more than sweetness bound me,
A spirit stirred;
Shadowy and cold it neared me,
Then shrank as if it feared me—
But 'twas I that feared.

TEN O'CLOCK NO MORE [1]

The wind has thrown
The boldest of trees down.
Now disgraced it lies,
Naked in spring beneath the drifting skies,
Naked and still.

It was the wind
So furious and blind
That scourged half England through,
Ruining the fairest where most fair it grew
By dell and hill.

And springing here,
The black clouds dragging near,
Against this lonely elm
Thrust all his strength to maim and overwhelm
In one wild shock.

As in the deep
Satisfaction of dark sleep
The tree her dream dreamed on,
And woke to feel the wind's arms round her thrown
And her head rock.

And the wind raught
Her ageing boughs and caught
Her body fast again.
Then in one agony of age, grief, pain,
She fell and died.

Her noble height,
Branches that loved the light,
Her music and cool shade,
Her memories and all of her is dead
On the hill side.

But the wind stooped.
With madness tired, and drooped
In the soft valley and slept.
While morning strangely round the hush'd tree crept
And called in vain.

The birds fed where
The roots uptorn and bare
Thrust shameful at the sky;
And pewits round the tree would dip and cry
With the old pain.

"Ten o'clock's gone!"
Said sadly every one.
And mothers looking thought
Of sons and husbands far away that fought:—
And looked again.

FROM WEAR TO THAMES

Is it because Spring now is come
That my heart leaps in its bed of dust?
Is it with sorrow or strange pleasure
To watch the green time's gathering treasure?

Or is there some too sharp distaste
In all this quivering green and gold?
Something that makes bare boughs yet barer,
And the eye's pure delight the rarer?

Not that the new found Spring is sour....
The blossom swings on the cherry branch,
From Wear to Thames I have seen this greenness
Cover the six-months-winter meanness.

And windflowers and yellow gillyflowers
Pierce the astonished earth with light:
And most-loved wallflower's bloody petal
Shakes over that long frosty battle.

But this leaping, sinking heart
Finds question in grass, bud and blossom—
Too deeply into the earth is prying,
Too sharply hears old voices crying.

There is in blossom, bud and grass
Something that's neither sorrow nor joy,
Something that sighs like autumn sighing,
And in each living thing is dying.

It is myself that whispers and stares
Down from the hill and in the wood,
And in the untended orchard's shining
Sees the light through thin leaves declining.

Let me forget what I have been
What I can never be again.
Let me forget my winter's meanness
In this fond, flushing world of greenness.

Let me forget the world that is

The changing image of my thought,
Nor see in thicket and hedge and meadow
Myself, a grave perplexèd shadow;

And O, forget that gloomy shade
That breathes his cloud 'twixt earth and light ...
All, all forget but sun and blossom,
And the bird that bears heaven in his bosom.

TIME FROM HIS GRAVE

When the south-west wind came
The air grew bright and sweet, as though a flame
Had cleansed the world of winter. The low sky
As the wind lifted it rose trembling vast and high,
And white clouds sallied by
As children in their pleasure go
Chasing the sun beneath the orchard's shadow and snow.
Nothing, nothing was the same!
Not the dull brick, not the stained London stone,
Not the delighted trees that lost their moan—
Their moan that daily vexed me with such pain
Until I hated to see trees again;
Nor man nor woman was the same
Nor could be stones again,
Such light and colour with the south-west came.
As I drank all that brightness up I saw
A dark globe lapt in fold on fold of gloom,
With all her hosts asleep in that cold tomb,
Sealed by an iron law.
And there amid the hills,
Locked in an icy hollow lay the bones
Of one that ghostly and enormous slept
Obscure 'neath wrinkled ice and bedded stones.
But as spring water the old dry channel fills,
Came the south-west wind filling all the air.
Then Time rose up, ghostly, enormous, stark,
With cold gray light in cold gray eyes, and dark
Dark clouds caught round him, feet to rigid chin.
The wind ran flushed and glorious in,
Godlike from hill to frozen hill-top stepp'd,
And swiftly upon that bony stature swept.
Then a long breath and then quick breaths I heard,
In those black caves of stillness music stirred,
Those icy heights were riven:
From crown to clearing hollow grass was green;

And godlike from flushed hill to hill-top leapt
Time, youthful, quick, serene,
Dew flashing from his limbs, light from his eyes
To the sheeny skies.
A lark's song climbed from earth and dropped from heaven,
Far off the tide clung to the shore
Now silent nevermore.
... Into what vision'd wonder was I swept,
Upon what unimaginable joyance had I leapt!

WILDER MUSIC

Came the same cuckoo's cry
All day across the mead.
Flitted the butterfly
All day dittering over my head.
Came a bleak crawk-caw
Between tall broad trees.
Came shadows, floating, drifting slowly down
Large leaves from darker trees.

Rose the lark with the rising sun,
Rose the mist after the lark,
O wild and sweet the clamour begun
Round the heels of the limping dark.
Rose after white cloud white cloud,
Nodded green cloud to green;
The stiff and dark earth stirred, breathing aloud,
And dew shook from the green.

Remained the eyes that stared,
Ears that ached to hear;
Remained the nerve of being, bared,
Stung with delight and fear.
Beauty flushed, ran and returned,
Like a music rose and fell;
Staring and blind and deaf I listened and burned—
A wilder music fell.

GRASSES

O cover me, long gentle grasses,
Cover me with your seeding heads,
Cover me with your shaking limbs,

Cover me with your light soft hands,
Cover me as the delicious long wind passes
Over you and me, green grasses.

'Tis of your blood I would be drinking,
To your soft shrilling listening now,
And your thin fingers peering through
At the deep forests of the sky.
O satisfy my peevish thought past thinking,
My sense with your sense linking.

Already are your brown roots creeping
Around the roots of my mind's mind,
Into the darkness hidden within
The rayed dark of unconsciousness;
And your long stems in a bright wind are leaping
Over me uneasily sleeping.

O cover me, long gentle grasses,
As one day over a quiet flesh
You will shake, shake and dance and sing;
And body too still and spirit astir
Will hear you in every firm bright wind that passes
Over you, loved green grasses.

FAIR AND BRIEF

So fair, that all the morning aches
With such monotony!
So brief, that sadness breaks
The brittle spell.

Nothing so fair, nothing so brief:
The sun leaps up and falls.
The wind tosses every leaf:
Every leaf dies.

Blossom, a white cloud in the air,
Is blown like a cloud away.
Must all be brief, being fair?
Nothing remain?

Yes, night and that high regiment
Of stars that wheel and march,
Ever their bright lines bent
To a secret thought;

Moving immutable, bright and grave,
Fair beyond all things fair;
Though all else vanish, save
Imagination's dream.

NIGHTFALL

I

Eve goes slowly
Dancing lightly
Clad with shadow up the hills;
Birds their singing
Cease at last, and silence
Falling like fine rain the valley fills.

Not a bat's cry
Stirs the stillness
Perfect as broad water sleeping,
Not a moth's wings
Flit in the gathering darkness,
Not a mouselike moonray ev'n comes creeping.

Then a light shines
From the casement,
Wreathed with jasmine boughs and stars,
Palely golden
As the late eve's primrose,
Glimmers through green leafy prison bars.

II

Only joy now
Come in silence,
Come before your look's forgot;
Come and hearken
While the lonely shadow
Broadens on the hill and then is not.

Now the hour is,
Here the place is,
Here am I who saw thee here.
Evening darkens
All is still and marvellous,
Now the sharp stars in the deep sky peer.

Come and fill me
As the wind fills
Leafy wide boughs of a tree;
Come and windlike
Cleanse my slumbrous branches,
Come and moonlike bathe the leaves of me.

III

Eve has gone and
Night follows,
Every bush is now a ghost;
Every tree looms
Lofty large and sombre;
All day's simple friendliness is lost.

See the poplars
Black in blackness,
In all their leaves there is no sigh.
'Neath that darkling
Cedar who dare wander
Now, or under the vast oak would lie!...

Till that tingling
Silence broken
Every clod renews its breath;
Birds, leaves, grasses
Heave as one, then sleep on
Full of sweeter sleep and unlike death.

IV

Only joy now
Come like music
Falling clear from strings of light;
Come like shadow
Drinking up late sunrays,
Come like moonrays sweeping the round night.

See how night is
Opening flowerlike:
Open so thy bosom to me.
See how earth falls
Easeful into silence:
Let my moth-wing'd thought so fall on thee.

While the lamp's beam

Primrose golden
Now is like a shifting spear
Borne in battle,
Seen awhile then hidden,
Bold then beaten—now long lost, and here!

THE SLAVES

The tall slaves bow if that capricious King
But glances as he passes;
Their dark hoods drawing over abashed faces
They bow humbly, unappealingly.
The dark robes round their shuddering bodies cling,
They bow and but whisper as he passes.

They have not learned to look into his eyes,
If he insults to answer,
To stand with head erect and angry arching bosom:
They bow humbly, unappealingly,
As though he mastered earth and the violet inky skies,
And whisper piteously for only answer.

So they stand, tall slaves, ashamed of their great height,
And if he comes raving,
Shouting from the west, furious and moody,
They bow more humbly, unappealingly,
Ashamed to remember how they lived in that calm light;
They droop until he passes, tired of raving.

Only when he's gone they lift their darkened brows,
Light comes back to their eyes,
Their leaves caress the light, the light laves their branches,
They move loverlike, appealingly;
Slaves now no more the poplars lift and shake their boughs,
And there's a heaven of evening in their eyes.

THE FUGITIVE

In the hush of early even
The clouds came flocking over,
Till the last wind fell from heaven
And no bird cried.

Darkly the clouds were flocking,

Shadows moved and deepened,
Then paused; the poplar's rocking
Ceased; the light hung still

Like a painted thing, and deadly.
Then from the cloud's side flickered
Sharp lightning, thrusting madly
At the cowering fields.

Thrice the fierce cloud lighten'd,
Down the hill slow thunder trembled;
Day in her cave grew frightened,
Crept away, and died.

THE UNTHRIFT

Here in the shade of the tree
The hours go by
Silent and swift,
Lightly as birds fly.
Then the deep clouds broaden and drift,
Or the cloudless darkness and the worn moon.
Waking, the dreamer knows he is old,
And the day that he dreamed was gone
Is gone.

THE WREN

Within the greenhouse dim and damp
The heat floats like a cloud.
Pale rose-leaves droop from the rust roof
With rust-edged roses bowed.
As I go in
Out flies the startled wren.

By the tall dark fir tree he sings
Morn after morn still,
Shy and bold he flits and sings
Tinily sweet and shrill.
As I go out
His song follows me about ...

About the orchard under trees
Beaded with cherries bright,

Past the rat-haunted Honeybourne
And up those hills of light:
As up I go
His notes more sweetly flow.

Or down those dark hills when night's there
Full of dark thoughts and deep,
A thin clear soundless music comes
Like stars in broken sleep.
When I come down
All those dark thoughts are flown.

And now that sweetness is more sweet,
Here where the aeroplanes
Labouring and groaning in the height
Lift their lifeless vans:—
Sweet, sweet to hear
The far off wren singing clear.

THE WINDS

In these green fields, in this green spring,
In this green world of burning sweet
That drives its sour from everything
And burns the Arctic with new heat,
That seems so slow and flies so fleet
On half-seen wing;

In this green world the birds are all
With motion mad, are wild with song;
The grass leaps like a sudden wall
Flung up against a foe that long
Strode round and wrought his frosty wrong.
The bright winds call,

The bright winds answer; the clouds rise
White from the grave, shaking their head,
Strewing the grave-clothes through the skies,
In languid drifting shadow shed
Upon the fields where, slowly spread,
Each shadow dies.

In every wood is green and gold,
The unbridged river runs all green
With queenly swan-clouds floating bold
Down to the mill's swift guillotine.

Beyond the mill each murdered queen
Floats white and cold.

—If I could rise up in a cloud
And look down on the new earth in flight,
Shadow-like cast my thought's thin shroud
Back upon these fields of light;
And hear the winds of day and night
Meet, singing loud!

THE WANDERER

Over the pool of sleep
The night mists creep,
Then faint thin light and then clear day,
Noontide, and lingering afternoon;
Then that Wanderer, the Moon
Wandering her old wild way.

How many spirits follow
Her in that dark hollow!
Like a lost lamb she roams on high
Through the cold and soundless sky,
And stares down into her deep
Reflection in the pool of sleep.

How many follow
Her in that lone hollow!
She sees them not nor would she hear
Though both shape and sound were clear,
But stares, stares into the pool
Of her fear and beauty full.

Far in strange gay skies
She pales and dies,
Forgetting that bright transitory
Reflection of astonished glory,
Nor heeds the spirits that follow
Her into day's bright hollow.

MERRILL'S GARDEN

There is a garden where the seeded stems of thin long grass are bowed
Beneath July's slow rains and heat and tired children's trailing feet;

And the trees' neglected branches droop and make a cloud beneath the cloud,
And in that dark the crimson dew of raspberries shines more sweet than sweet.

The flower of the tall acacia's gone, the acacia's flower is white no more,
The aspen lifts his pithless arms, the aspen leaves are close and still;
The wind that tossed the clouds along, gray clouds and white like feathers bore,
Lets even a feather faintly fall and smoke spread hugely where it will.

But though the acacia's flower is gone and raspberries bear bright fruit untasted,
Beauty lives there, oh rich and rare, past the sum of eager June.
The lime tree's pyramid of flower and leaf and yellow flower unwasted
Rises at eve and bars the breast wild-heaving of the timid moon.

Now the tall pear-trees unrebuked lift their green fingers to the sky;
Their lower boughs are crossed like arms of templars in long stony sleep.
Their arms are crossed as though the wind, returning from wild war on high,
Had touched them with an angry breath, or whispered from his cavern deep.

A foxglove lifts her bells and bells silent above the singing grass,
Still the old marigold her light sprinkles like riches to the poor.
Snapdragon still his changeling blossom shakes with the burden of the bees,
And the strong bindweed creeps and winds and springs on high a conqueror.

Would now her eyes grieve to behold snapdragon, foxglove, marigold
Daily diminish in their sweet and bindweed wreathing over all—
Weed and grass and weed and grass, friendless, melancholy, cold,
Wreathing the earth like wreathing snow from bare wall to low greening wall?

Old were her eyes that lingered on old trees and grass and flowers trim.
She smelt the ripe pears when they drooped and fell and broke upon the path.
Old were her thoughts of things of old; her present thoughts were few and dim;
Her eyes saw not the things she saw; she listened, to no living breath.

Her youth and prime and autumn time bloomed in her thought all light and sweet:
No wallflower more of sweet could hold, of sunny light no marigold.
Fruit on her mind's boughs ripened full, in summer's and calm autumn's heat:
Then fell, for there came none to pick; but winter came, and she was old.

Now if her sons come they will find—not her: her empty garden only,
The wallflower done and snapdragon still swinging with the greedy bees,
Marigold glittering in the grass, scant foxglove ringing faintly, lonely,
Close red fruit beading the long boughs and bindweed wreathing where it please.

A tawny lean cat Marmalade slinks like a panther through the tall
Thin bending grass and watches long a scholar thrush rehearsing song;
Or children running in the sun hunt and hunt a well lost ball;
But most the garden sleeps away the day, but still, when eves are long,

When eves are long and no moon rises, and nervous, still, is all the air,
That small stiff figure moves again, silent amid the hushing grass;
In the firm-carven lime tree's shade she moves, and meets her old thoughts there,
Then in the deepening dark is lost, or her light steps unnoted pass.

Only that careless garden keeps secure her memory though it sleeps,
And the bright flowers and tyrant weed and tall grass shaking its loud seed
Less lovely were if wanting her who like a living thought still creeps
And sees what once she saw and music hears of her living sons and dead.

THE LIME TREE

That lime tree on the distant rising ground
(If it was a lime tree) showed her yellow leaves
Above the renewed green of wet August grass—
First Autumn yellow that on first Autumn eves
Too soon was found.

Comfortless lime tree! Scarce an aspen leaf
Like a green butterfly flitted to the ground;
There was no sign of Autumn in the grass.
Even the long garden beds their beauty brief—
Their mignonette,

Nasturtium and sweet-william and red stocks,
And clover crouching in the border grass,
And blood-like fuschia, eve's primrose and white phlox
And honeysuckle—waved all their smell and hue
Morn and eve anew.

But that far lime tree yellowing by the oak,
Warning oak, elm and poplar and each fresh tree
Shaking in the south wind delightedly,
And clover in the closeness of the grass,
Warns also me.

And now when all the trees are standing still
Beneath the purple and white of the west sky,
And time is standing still—as stand it will—
That early yellowing lime with palsied fingers
Cannot be still.

DARK CHESTNUT

Thou shaking thy dark shadows down,
Like leaves before the first leaves fall,
Pourest upon the head of night
Her loveliest loveliness of all—
Dark leaves that tremble
When soft airs unto softer call.

O, darker, softer fall her thoughts
Upon the cold fields of my mind,
Weaving a quiet music there
Like leaf-shapes trembling in least wind:
Dark thoughts that linger
When the light's gone and the night's blind.

I see her there beneath your boughs.
Dark chestnut, though you see her not;
Her white face and white hands are clear
As the moon in your stretched arms caught;
But stranger, clearer,
The living shadows of her thought.

LONELY AIRS

Ah, bird singing late in the gloam
While the evening shadow thickens,
And the dizzy bat-wings roam,
And the faint starlight quickens;

And her bud eve's primrose bares
Before night's cold fingers come:
Thine are such lonely airs,
Bird singing late in the gloam!

THE CREEPER

It covered all
The cold east wall,
Its green, thin gold, purple, brown,
And flame running up and down;
Lifting its quiet bosom to every wind that crept
Up the high wall and in its darkness slept.
Then when the wind slept all the creeper turned
To undiminishing fire that burned and burned and burned.

But one black night
(For not in the light
May such treacheries be done)
Came with dishonoured weapon one
And cut the stem just where the branches thin
Their million-leaf'd wild wandering begin:
Cut the firm stem quite through, and so it bled,
And all the million leaves shivered and hung there dead.

The wall how cold,
The house how old
Became when that warm bright fire died,
And the fond wind could no more hide.
And it was strange that so much death could be
From one dark night-hour's darker felony;
And how the leaves being dead could not cast down
Their colours in bright pools of red and gold and brown.

—It did not die,
But flamed on high
Morn after morn, even when white snow
Covered all brightness, high and low;
And in the night when the snow glimmered wan
Still beautiful as a fire its brightness shone:
Its million quiet leaves quivering in my mind,
When from no earthly meadows crept the remembered wind.

SMOKE

They stood like men that hear immortal speech
Moving among their branches, and like trees
We stood and watched them, and in our still branches
Echoes of that immortal music stirred.
October days had touched their breasts with light,
With yellow light and red light and wan green;
And the gray cloud that grew from low to high
Made the warm light more warm, the green more wan.
We stood and watched them and in our still branches
We felt the warm light glow, though now the rain
Was loud upon the leaves.
And standing there
You cried, "O, that sweet smell, where is the fire?
Where is the fire?" For sharp upon the rain
The smell came of a wood fire and clung round
Hanging upon our branches, till we saw
No more those lighted trees nor heard the rain—

Knew only the deep echoes and the smell
Of a wood fire that breathed its smoke across
From some near hearth, or undiscovered world.

QUEENS

The red sun stared unwinking at the East
Then slept under a cloak of hodden gray;
The rimy fields held the last light of day,
A little tender yet. And I remember
How black against the pale and wintry west
Stood the confused great army of old trees,
Topping that lean, enormous-shouldered hill
With crossing lances shivering and then still.
I looked as one that sees
Queens passing by and lovelier than he dreamed,
With fringe of silver light following their feet,
And all those lances vail'd, and solemn Knights
Watching their Queens as with eyes grave and sweet
They left for the gray fields those airy heights.
Nothing had lovelier seemed—
Not April's noise nor the early dew of June,
Nor the calm languid cow-eyed Autumn Moon,
Nor ruffling woods the greenest I remember—
Than this pale light and dark of cold December.

THE RED HOUSE

On the wide fields the water gleams like snow,
And snow like water pale beneath pale sky,
When old and burdened the white clouds are stooped low.
Sudden as thought, or startled near bird's cry,
The whiteness of first light on hills of snow
New dropped from skiey hills of tumbling white
Streams from the ridge to where the long woods lie;
And tall ridge-trees lift their soft crowns of white
Above slim bodies all black or flecked with snow.
By the tossed foam of the not yet frozen brook
Black pigs go straggling over fields of snow;
The air is full of snow, and starling and rook
Are blacker amid the myriad streams of light.
Warm as old fire the Red House burns yet bright
Beneath the unmelting snows of pine and larch,
While February moves as slow, as slow

As Spring might never come, never come March.

Amid such snows, by generations haunted,
By echoes, memories and dreams enchanted,
Firm when dark winds through the night stamp and shout,
Brightest when time silvers the world all about,
That old house called The Heart burns, burns, and still
Outbraves the mortal threat of the hanging hill.

THE BEAM

The dead white on the fields' dead white
Turned the peace to misery.
Tall bony trees their wild arms thrust
Into the cold breast of the night.
Brightly the stars shone in their dust.
The hard wind's gust
Scratched like a bird the frozen snow.

Against the dead light grew the gold,
Lifting its beam to that high dust;
The lamp within the hut's small pane
Called the world to life again.
Arms of the trees atremble thrust
Defiance at the cold
Night of narrow shrouding snow.

A human beam, small spear of light,
Lifting its beauty to that high
Indifference of starry dust.
The aching trees were comforted,
And their brave arms more deeply thrust
Into the sky.
Earth's warm light fingered the dead snow.

LAST HOURS

A gray day and quiet,
With slow clouds of gray,
And in dull air a cloud that falls, falls
All day.

The naked and stiff branches
Of oak, elm, thorn,

In the cold light are like men aged and
Forlorn.

Only a gray sky,
Grass, trees, grass again,
And all the air a cloud that drips, drips,
All day.

Lovely the lonely
Bare trees and green grass—
Lovelier now the last hours of slow winter
Slowly pass.

THE WISH

That you might happier be than all the rest,
Than I who have been happy loving you,
Of all the innocent even the happiest—
This I beseeched for you.

Until I thought of those unending skies—
Of stagnant cloud, or fleckless dull blue air,
Of days and nights delightless, no surprise,
No threat, no sting, no fear;

And of the stirless waters of the mind,
Waveless, unfurrowed, of no living hue,
With dead eaves dropping slowly in no wind,
And nothing flowering new.

And then no more I wished you happiness,
But that whatever fell of joy or woe
I would not dare, O Sweet, to wish it less,
Or wish you less than you.

NOWHERE, EVERYWHERE

Flesh and blood, bone and skin,
Are the house that beauty lives in.
Formed in darkness, grown in light
Are they the substance of delight.
Who could have dreamed the things he sees
In these strong lovely presences—
In cheeks of children, thews of men,

Women's bodies beloved of men?
Who could have dreamed a thing so wise
As that clear look of the child's eyes?
Who the thin texture of her hand
But with a hand's touch understand?
Shaped in eternity were these
Body's miracles, where the seas
Their continuous rhythm learned,
And the stars in their bright order burned.
From stars and seas was motion caught
When flesh, blood, bone and skin were wrought
Into swift lovely liveliness.
Oh, but beauty less and less
Than beauty grows. The cheeks fall in,
Colour dies from the smooth skin,
And muscles slack and bones are brittle;
Veins and arteries little by little
Delay the tides of the blood:
That is a ditch that was a flood.
Then all but dry bones disappears,
White bones that lie a hundred years
Cheated of resurrection....
Where is that beauty gone?
Escaped even while we watched it so,
And none guessed the way it would go?
Only it's fled, and here alone
Lie blood and skin and flesh and bone.
Where is the beauty that was here?
—Nowhere, everywhere.

TAKE CARE, TAKE CARE

Bind up, bind up your dark bright hair
And hide the smouldering sunken fire.
Let it be held no more than fair,
Nor yourself guess how rare, how rare
Its movement, colour and deep fire.

Your eyes they have their consciousness,
Your lips their grave reflective smile,
Your hands their cunning for distress:
Your hair has only beauteousness
And hid flame for its only guile.

That glowing hair on shoulders white
Is pride past sum: take care, take care!

Even to dream of wish'd delight
Too much perturbs the ebb of night—
Bind up, bind up your burning hair!

NEARNESS

Thy hand my hand,
Thine eyes my eyes,
All of thee
Caught and confused with me:
My hand thy hand
My eyes thine eyes,
All of me
Sunken and discovered anew in thee....

No: still
A foreign mind,
A thought
By other yet uncaught;
A secret will
Strange as the wind:
The heart of thee
Bewildering with strange fire the heart in me.

Hand touches hand,
Eye to eye beckons,
But who shall guess
Another's loneliness?
Though hand grasp hand
Though the eye quickens,
Still lone as night
Remain thy spirit and mine, past touch and sight.

THE SECOND FLOOD

How could I know, how could I guess
That here was your great happiness—
In mine? And how could I know
Your love infinite must grow?

Suddenly at dawn I wake
To see the cruse of colour break
Over the East, and then the gray
Creep up with light of common day ...

No, no, no! again that bright
Flashing, flushing, flooding light
Leading on day, until I ache
With love to see the dark world wake.

O, with such second flood your love
Painted my earth and heaven above,
With such wild magnificence
As bruised my heart in every sense,
In every nerve. Was ever man
Fit this renewed love to sustain?

Now in these days when Autumn's leaf
Is red and gold, and for a brief
Day the earth flowers ere it dies,
What if Spring came with new surprise,
Came ere the aspen shivered bare
Or the beech coins glittered in cold air,
Before the rough wind the maple stripped
And this bare moon on bare boughs stepped!
Vain thought—O, yet not wholly vain:
Even to me Love has come again,
Moving from your quick breast where he
Fluttered in his wondering infancy.

THE GLASS

Your fce has lost
The clearness it once wore,
And your brow smooth and white
Its look of light;
Your eyes that were
So careless, are how deep with care!

O, what has done
This cruelty to you?
Is it only Time makes strange
Your look with change,
Or something more
Than the worst pang Time ever bore?—

Regret, regret!
So bitter that it changes
Bright youth to madness,
Poisoning mere sadness ...
O, vain glass that shows

Less than the bitterness the heart knows.

BUT MOST THY LIGHT

I know how fire burns,
How from the wrangling fumes
Rose and amber blooms,
And slowly dies.

Nothing's so swift as fire,
There's nothing alive so fierce.
The lifted lances pierce,
Sink, and upspring.

Like an Indian sword it leaps
Out of the smoking sheath.
Even the winged feet of death
Learn speed from fire;

And pain its cunning learns;
Languor its sweet
From the decaying heat
That never dies.

I know how fire burns
Unguessed, save for tears,
When the thousand-fanged flame spears
The body's guard;

Or when the mind, the mind
Is ever-glowing wood,
And fire runs in the blood
Lunatic, blind;

When remorse burns and burns
And burns always, always—
The fire that surest slays
Or surest numbs.

I know how fire burns
But how I cannot tell.
And Heaven burns like Hell
Yet the Heart endures.

'Tis the immortal Flame
In mortal life that's bitter,

Or than all sweet sweeter
Though life burns down.

Teach me, fire, but this,
Nor alone destroying burn:—
Of thy warmth let me learn,
But most thy light.

IN THAT DARK SILENT HOUR

In that dark silent hour
When the wind wants power,
And in the black height
The sky wants light,
Stirless and black
In utter lack,
And not a sound
Escapes from that untroubled round:—

To wake then
In the dark, and ache then
Until the dark is gone—
Lonely, yet not alone;
Hearing another's breath
All the quiet beneath,
Knowing one sleeps near
That day held dear

And dreams held dear; but now
In this sharp moment—how
Share the moment's sweetness,
Forgo its completeness,
Nor be alone
Now the dark is grown
Spiritual and deep
More than in dreams and sleep?

O, it is pain, 'tis need
That so wlll plead
For a little loneliness.
If it be pain to miss
Loved touch, look and lip,
Companionship
Yet is verier pain
Then, then

In that dark silent hour
When the wind wants power,
And you, near or far, sleep,
And your released thoughts toward me creep
While I, imprisoned, awake,
Ache—ache
To be for one
Long, little moment with myself alone.

ONCE THERE WAS TIME

Let no tears fall
If then they fell not.
If eyes told nothing,
Now let them tell not.
Once there was time
For words, looks and tears:
That time is past, is past—
Heart, thou shalt tell not!

Beyond any speech
Is silence bitter,
As between love and love
Nothing is sweeter.
Once there was time, time yet
For words, looks and tears ...
Past, past, past, past—
Nothing so bitter!

Now if tears come
That then fell never;
If eyes such sad, sad things
Look now for ever;
If words, looks or tears
Tremble with telling,
Oh, what returning voice is it whispers
Never, never, never!

SCATTER THE SILVER ASH LIKE SNOW

O, what insect is it
That burrows in the heart and frets
The heart's near nerves,
Leaving its unclean

Stigmata in the mind serene,
Making the proud how mean?

It is not common hate,
Anger has not such deadly cunning
To annul, to chill.
Wild anger is not
So cunning even while so hot;
Hate is too soon forgot.

There is no sword so sharp
With lightnings as the wanton tongue;
Nothing that burns like words—
Bubbling flames that spread
In the now unspiritual head,
By sleepless fevers fed.

O evil words that are
The knives of desolating thought!
And though words be still
The hot eyes yet dart
Burning deaths from this mad heart
Into that torn heart.

O Love, forget, forget,
Put by that glittering edge, put by;
Slay the insect with light;
Smother that smoky glow,
Scatter the silver ash like snow
When thy spring airs blow!

JUSTIFICATION

From far-off it came near
Deep-charactered and clear,
Until I saw the features close to mine
And the eyes unhappy shine.

It was Sorrow's face,
Wanting kindness and grace,
And wanting strength of silence, and the power
To abide a luckier hour.

The first fear turned to hating
As I saw him dumbly waiting,
For it was my true likeness that he wore

And would wear evermore:—

My face that was to be
When his years' misery
With here a little and there a little had made
My strong spirit afraid.

I saw his face and hated,
Seeing mine so sad-fated.
And then I struck and killed him, knowing that he
Had else slain me.

I HAVE NEVER LOVED YOU YET

I have never loved you yet, if now I love.

If Love was born in that bright April sky
And ran unheeding when the sun was high,
And slept as the moon sleeps through Autumn nights
While those dear steady stars burn in their heights:

If Love so lived and ran and slept and woke
And ran in beauty when each morning broke,
Love yet was boylike, fervid and unstable,
Teased with romance, not knowing truth from fable.

But Winter after Autumn comes and stills
The petulant waters and the wild mind fills
With silence; and the dark and cold are bitter,
O, bitter to remember past days sweeter.

Then Spring with one warm cloudy finger breaks
The frost and the heart's airless black soil shakes;
Love grown a man uprises, serious, bright
With mind remembering now things dark and light.

O, if young Love was beautiful, Love grown old
Experienced and grave is not grown cold.
Life's faithful fire in Love's heart burns the clearer
With all that was, is and draws darkling nearer.

I have never loved you yet, if now I love.

THE PIGEONS

The pigeons, following the faint warm light,
Stayed at last on the roof till warmth was gone,
Then in the mist that's hastier than night
Disappeared all behind the carved dark stone,
Huddling from the black cruelty of the frost.
With the new sparkling sun they swooped and came
Like a cloud between the sun and street, and then
Like a cloud blown from the blue north were lost,
Vanishing and returning ever again,
Small cloud following cloud across the flame
That clear and meagre burned and burned away
And left the ice unmelting day by day.

... Nor could the sun through the roof's purple slate
(Though his gold magic played with shadow there
And drew the pigeons from the streaming air)
With any fiery magic penetrate.
Under the roof the air and water froze,
And no smoke from the gaping chimney rose.
The silver frost upon the window-pane
Flowered and branched each starving night anew,
And stranger, lovelier and crueller grew;
Pouring her silver that cold silver through,
The moon made all the dim flower bright again.

... Pouring her silver through that barren flower
Of silver frost, until it filled and whitened
A room where two small children waited, frightened
At the pale ghost of light that hour by hour
Stared at them till though fear slept not they slept.
And when that white ghost from the window crept,
And day came and they woke and saw all plain,
Though still the frost-flower blinded the window-pane,
And touched their mother and touched her hand in vain,
And wondered why she woke not when they woke;
And wondered what it was their sleep that broke
When hand in hand they stared and stared, so frightened;
They feared and waited, and waited all day long
While all the shadows went and the day brightened,
All the ill shadows but one shadow strong.

Outside were busy feet and human speech
And daily cries and horns. Maybe they heard,
Painfully wondering still, and each to each
Leaning, and listening if their mother stirred—
Cold, cold,
Hungering as the long slow hours grew old,

Though food within the cupboard idle lay
Beyond their thought, or but beyond their reach.
The soft blue pigeons all the afternoon
Sunned themselves on the roof or rose at play,
Then with the shrinking light fluttered away;
And once more came the icy hearted moon,
Staring down at the frightened children there
That could but shiver and stare.

... How many hours, how many days, who knows?
Neighbours there were who thought they had gone away
To return some luckier or luckless day.
No sound came from the room: the cold air froze
The very echo of the children's sighs.
And what they saw within each other's eyes,
Or heard each other's heart say as they peered
At the dead mother lying there, and feared
That she might wake, and then might never wake,
Who knows, who knows?
None heard a living sound their silence break.

In those cold days and nights how many birds
Flittering above the fields and streams all frozen
Watched hungrily the tended flocks and herds—
Earth's chosen nourished by earth's wise self-chosen!
How many birds suddenly stiffened and died
With no plaint cried,
The starved heart ceasing when the pale sun ceased!
And when the new day stepped from the same cold East
The dead birds lay in the light on the snow-flecked field,
Their song and beautiful free winging stilled.

I walked under snow-sprinkled hills at night,
And starry sprinkled, skies deep blue and bright.
The keen wind thrust with his knife against the thin
Breast of the wood as I went tingling by
And heard a weak cheep-cheep—no more—the cry
Of a bird that crouched the smitten wood within....
But no one heeded that sharp spiritual cry
Of the two children in their misery,
When in the cold and famished night death's shade
More terrible the moon's cold shadows made.
How was it none could hear
That bodiless crying, birdlike, sharp and clear?

I cannot think what they, unanswered, thought
When the night came again and shadows moved
As the moon through the ice-flower stared and roved,

And that unyielding Shadow came again.
That Shadow came again unseen and caught
The children as they sat listening in vain,
Their starved hearts failing ere the Shadow removed.
And when the new morn stepped from the same cold East
They lay unawakening in the barren light,
Their song and their imaginations bright,
Their pains and fears and all bewilderment ceased....
While the brief sun gave
New beauty to the death-flower of the frost,
And pigeons in the frore air swooped and tossed,
And glad eyes were more glad and grave less grave.

There is not pity enough in heaven or earth,
There is not love enough, if children die
Like famished birds—oh, less mercifully.
A great wrong's done when such as these go forth
Into the starless dark, broken and bruised,
With mind and sweet affection all confused,
And horror closing round them as they go.
There is not pity enough!

And I have made, children, these verses for you,
Lasting a little longer than your breath,
Because I have been haunted with your death;
So men are driven to things they hate to do.
Jesus, forgive us all our happiness,
As Thou dost blot out all our miseries.

AND THESE FOR YOU

I

NOT WITH THESE EYES

Let me not see your grief!
O, let not any see
That grief,
Nor how your heart still rocks
Like a temple with long earthquake shocks.
Let me not see
Your grief.

These eyes have seen such wrong,
Yet remained cold:
Ills grown strong,

Corruption's many-headed worm
Destroying feet that moved so firm—
Shall these eyes see
Your grief?

And that black worm has crawled
Into the brain
Where thought had walked
Nobly, and love and honour moved as one,
And brave things bravely were begun....
Now, can thought see
Unabashed your grief?

Into that brain your grief
Has run like cleansing fire:
Your grief
Through these unfaithful eyes has leapt
And touched honour where it lightly slept.
Now when I see
In memory your grief

There is no thought that's not
Yours, yours,
No love that sleeps,
No spiritual door that opens not
In the green quiet village of thought
Shining with light,
And silent to your silence.

II

ASKING FORGIVENESS

I did not say, "Yes, we had better part
Since love is over or must be suppressed."
I did not say, "I'll hold you in my heart
Saint-like, and in the thought of your thought rest,
And pray for you and wish you happiness
In a better love than mine."

I was another man to another woman,
Tears falling or burnt dry were nothing then.
I struck your heart, I struck your mind; inhuman,
Future and past I stabbed and stabbed again,
Cursing the very thought of your happiness
In another love than mine:

—Then left you sick to death, and I like death.
It was a broken body bore me away—
A broken mind—poisoned by my own breath,
And love self-poisoned.... Was it but yesterday?
—Forgive, forgive, forgive, forgive, forgive,
Forgive!

JUDGMENT DAY

When through our bodies our two spirits burn
Escaping, and no more our true eyes turn
Outwards, and no more hands to fond hands yearn;

Then over those poor grassy heaps we'll meet
One morning, tasting still the morning's sweet,
Sensible still of light, dark, rain, cold, heat;

And see 'neath the green dust that dust of gray
Which was our useless bodies laid away,
Mocked still with menace of a Judgment Day.

We then that waiting dust at last will call,
Each to the other's,—"Rise up at last, O small
Ashes that first-love held loveliest of all!

"'Tis Judgment Day, arise!" And they will arise,
The dust will lift, and spine, ribs, neck, head, knees
At the sound remember their old unities,

And stand there, yours with mine, as once they stood
Beloved, obeyed, despised, with that swift blood,
Those looks and trembling lips, heart's pause and thud.

"And was it these that love-galled thought pursued
And with his immortality indued,
Nor was by their mortality quite subdued?

"This was the bony hand that held my hand,
The shoulders whereon all my world might stand:
They fell, but in their fall was I unmanned?

"This was the breast my eyes delighted in,
The ribs were faint as now under the skin:
They mouldered, but not my love mouldered within.

"Away, away! This was not truly thee—

A mortal bravery, Time's delinquency,
A dream that held me from thee, thee from me.

"It was not in these bodies that we drew
Near, nearer: never, never by these we knew
Transfusion past all sense of 'I' and 'You.'

"It was youth's blindness held the body so dear:
Slowly, slowly, year after bewildered year,
The dark thinned and the eyes of love grew clear,

"And thought following thought, enlinking each,
Ran where the delighting body could not reach,
And had speech when there was no voice for speech;

"So that we scarce grieved when those bodies died,
And our eyes more than our true spirits cried;
But as when trees fall, the free wind that sighed

"Awhile in their fond branches ceases not,
But sings a moment over the cumbered spot,
Then flies away:—our unentangled thought,

"Our vivid spirits of love, unbroken moved
And lifted no more sense-confined, and roved
And knew till then we had not utterly loved ...

"Leave now this dust!"

And then the dust will sink,
The upheaved mound to its old shape will shrink,
And we shall turn again from Time's dusk brink.

Will it be thus? It will be thus. Even now,
Though body to body submissively still bow,
'Tis not on body's blood that our loves grow.

Though I am old and you are old, though nerves
Slacken, and beauty slowly lose its curves,
And greedy Time the bone and sinew starves,

Like some lean Captain gloating over a town
That has not fallen, but will fall, every stone
O'erthrust and every bravery overthrown;

Who entering the defeated walls at last
Finds emptiness, and hears an escaping blast,
Triumphant from the shining east hills cast,

And knows defeat in victory.... O that rare
Music is ours, is ours—prelusive air
Caught from the Judgment music high and severe.

Will it indeed be thus? Yes, thus! The body burns,
Not with desire, and into pale smoke turns,
And there is only flame towards flame that yearns.

While that ill lecherous Time among the stones
Sits musing and rocking his old brittle bones,
Irked by long shadows, mocked by those bright far tones.

LIGHTING THE FIRE

You were a gipsy as you bent
Your dark hair over the black grate.
Hardly the west light above the hill
Showed your shadow, crooked and still.
The bellows hissed, and one bright spark
Deepened the hasty dark.

The bellows hissed, and the old smell
Crept on the air of smoking peat,
And round the spark a bubbling flame
Grew bright and loud. Sweeping the gloom
Lunatic shadows fled and came
Whirling about the room.

Then as you raised your head I saw
In the clear light of the bubbling fire
Your dark hair all lined with the gray
Sprinkled by years and sorrow and pain ...
Till as the bellows idle lay
Shadow swept back again.

RECOVERY

Where are you going with eyes so dull,
You whose eyes were beautiful,
You whose hair with the light was gay,
And now is thin and harsh and gray?
Is it age alone or age and tears
That has slowly rubbed your beauty away?

Where were you going when your swift eyes
Were like merry birds under May skies?—
In your cheeks the colours fluttering brave
As you danced with the wind and ran with the wave.
From what bright star was your brightness caught?
What to your music the music gave?

Now is your beauty a thing of old,
The fire is sunken, the ashes cold.
But if sweet singing on your ear stray,
Or the praise is uttered of yesterday,
Or of courage and nobleness one word said—
Like a cloud Time's ravage is brushed away.

EYES

A winter sky of pale blue and pale gold,
Bare trees, a wind that made the wood-path cold,
And one slow-moving figure, gray and old.

We met where the soft path falls from the wood
Down to the village. As I came near she stood
And answered when I spoke, drawing the hood

Back from her face. I saw only her eyes,
Large and sad. I could not bear those eyes.
They were like new graves. I could not bear her eyes.

But what we said as each passed on is gone.
We looked and spoke and passed like strangers on,
I to the high wood, she towards the paling sun.

And there, where the clear-heavened small pool lies,
And the tallest beeches brush the bending skies,
In pool and tree I saw again her eyes.

FULFILMENT

Happy are they whom men and women love,
And you were happy as a river that flows
Down between lonely hills, and knows
The pang and virtue of that loneliness,
And moves unresting on until it move

Under the trees that stoop at the low brink
And deepen their cool shade, and drink
And sing and hush and sing again,
Breathing their music's many-toned caress;
While the river with his high clear music speaks
Sometimes of loneliness, of hills obscure,
Sometimes of sunlight dancing on the plain,
Or of the night of stars unbared and deep
Multiplied in his depths unbared and pure;
Sometimes of winds that from the unknown sea creep,
Sometimes of morning when most clear it breaks
Spilling its brightness on his breast like rain:—
And then flows on in loneliness again
Towards the unknown near sea.
Was it in mere happiness or pain?
There were things said that spoke of naked pain,
With nothing between the wound and the sharp-edged world;
Things seen that told of such perplexity
As darkened night with night: but was that pain?
And there were things created all delight,
Making delight fruitful a hundred fold:
Sweetness of earth, energy of sun and rain,
Colour and shape, flowers and grasses bright,
And the clear firm body of a bare lovely hill,
And woods around its feet fast caught and curled,
And the cold sweets of lonely travelled night....
And was that happiness?—or something more,
That gathered happiness and pain like flowers
Half perished, and let them perish; and brightened still
In those dark mental journeys of cold hours
That found you what you were and left you stronger,
Shutting a door and opening a door?...
O door that you have passed so quickly through,
Ere we well knew what man you were, nor knew
What you had shown in life but a little longer!
It was not pain nor happiness for you,
Not any named delight or pang of sense,
But swift fulfilment past all sense or thought
Of what you were with all that time could make you;
No separate gift, spiritual influence,
But something wrought
From your own heart, with all that life could make you.

BRING YOUR BEAUTY

Bring your beauty, bring your laughter, bring even your fears,

Bring the grief that is, the joy that was in other years,
Bring again the happiness, bring love, bring tears.

There was laughter once, there were grave, happy eyes,
Talk of firm earth, old earth-sweeping mysteries:
There were great silences under clear dark skies.

Now is silence, now is loneliness complete; all is done.
The thrush sings at dawn, too sweet, up creeps the sun:
But all is silent, silent, for all that was is done.

Yet bring beauty and bring laughter, and bring even tears,
And cast them down; strew your happiness and fears,
Then leave them to the darkness of thought and years.

Fears in that darkness die; they have no spring.
Grief in that darkness is a bird that wants wing....
O love, love, your brightness, your beauty bring.

MEMORIAL

The wild October sky
Rises not so high,
The tree's roots that creep
Into the earth's body thrust not so deep
As our high and dark thought.

Yet thought need not roam
Far off to bring you home.
The sky is our wild mind,
Your roots are round our spirits twined,
To ours are your hearts caught.

O, never buried dead!
The living brain in the head
Is not so quick as you
Burning our conscious darkness through
With brightness past our thought.

THE HUMAN MUSIC

At evening when the aspens rustled soft
And the last blackbird by the hedge-nest laughed,
And through the leaves the moon's unmeaning face

Looked, and then rose in dark-blue leafless space;
Watching the trees and moon she could not bear
The silence and the presence everywhere.
The blackbird called the silence and it came
Closing and closing round like smoke round flame.
Into her heart it crept and the heart was numb,
Even wishes died, and all but fear was dumb—
Fear and its phantoms. Then the trees were enlarged,
And from their roundness unguessed shapes emerged,
Or no shape but the image of her fear
Creeping forth from her mind and hovering near.
If a bat flitted it was an evil thing;
Sadder the trees grew with every shadowy wing—
Their shape enlarged, their arms quivered, their thought
Stirring in the leaves a silent anguish wrought.
"What are they thinking of, the evil trees,
Nod-nodding, standing in malignant ease?
Something against man's mortal heart was sworn
Once, when their dark Powers were conceived and born;
And in such fading or such lightless hours
The world is delivered to these plotting Powers."
No physical swift blow she dreaded, not
Lightning's quick mercy; but her heart grew hot
And cold and hot with uncomprehended sense
Of an assassin spiritual influence
Moving in the unmoving trees....
Till, as she stared,
Her eyes turned cowards at last, and no more dared.
Yet could she never rise and shut the door:
Perhaps those Powers would batter at the door,
And that were madness. So right through the house
She set the doors all wide when she could arouse
The body's energy to serve the mind.
Then the air would move, and any little wind
Would cleanse awhile the darkness and diminish
Her fear, and the dumb shadow-war would finish.

But it was not the trees, the birds, the moon;
Birds cease, months fly, green seasons wither soon:
Nature was constant all the seasons through,
Sinister, watchful, and a thick cloud drew
Over the mind when its simplicity
Challenged what seemed with thought of what must be....
She wondered, seeing how a child could play
Lightly in a shady field all day:
For in that golden, brief, benignant weather
When spring and summer calling run together
And the sun's fresh and hot, she saw deep guile

In the sweetness of that unconditioned smile.
Sweetness not sweetness was but indifference
Or wantonness disguised, to her grave sense;
And if she could have seen the things she felt
She'd looked for darkness, and lit shapes that knelt
Appealing, unregarded, at a high
Altar uprising from the pit to the sky....
Had the trees consciousness, with flowers and clouds
And winds that hung like thin clouds in the woods,
And stars and silence:—had they each a mind
Bending on hers, clear eyes on her eyes blind?
In the green dense heights—elm, oak, ash, yew or beech
She scarce saw—was there not a brain in each,
An undiscovered centre of quick nerves
By which (like man) the tree lives, masters, serves,
Waxes and wanes? Oppressed her mind would shrink
From thought, and into her trembling body sink.

Something of this had childhood taught her when
Sickly she lay and peered again and again
At gray skies and white skies and void bright blue,
And watched the sun the bare town-tree boughs through,
And then through leafy boughs and once more bare.
Or in the west country's heavy hill-drawn air
Had felt the green grass pushing within her veins,
Tangling and strangling: and the warm spring rains
Tapping all night upon her childish head:
She shivered, lying lonely on her bed,
With all that life all round and she so weak,
Longing to speak—yet what was there to speak?
And as she grew and health came and love came
And life was happier, happier, still the same
Inhuman spirit rose whenever she
Held in her thoughts more than her eyes could see.
Behind the happiest hours the dark cloud hung
Distant or nearing, and its dullness flung
On the south meadows of her thought, the fairest
Shrinking in shadow; aspirations rarest
Falling, like shot birds in a reedy fen,
Slain by the old Enemy of men.
Life ebbed while men strove for the means of life;
The grudging earth turned labour into strife.
The moving hosts within the heavy clod
Seemed infinite in malice; frost and flood,
Season and inter-season, were conspired
In smiling or sour mockery; and untired
And undelighted, man scratched and scratched on,
And what he did, by Nature was undone.

She saw men twisted more than rocks or trees,
Bruised, numbed, by age and labour and the disease
Of labour in the cold fields; women worn
By many child-bearings, and their self-scorn
Because of time and their lost woman's powers.
Bitter was Nature to women; for those hours
Of the spirit's and the body's first delight
Passed soon, and the long day, evening, night
Of life uncherished; bitterest when even
That brief hour was denied, of dancing heaven,
Dewy love, and fulfilled desires.
But age
Of all ills made her pity and anger rage.
To see and smell the calm months bud and bloom,
April's first warmth, June's hues and slow perfume,
The sweetness drifting by in those long hours
While, out of her she nursed, the vital powers
Were pressed by pain and pressed by pain renewed,
Till, closing the life-long vicissitude,
Came starving death with full-heaped summer, and
Wrung the last pangs that spirit could withstand ...
Or to see age in its prison slowly freeze
With impotence more disastrous than disease,
While trees flowered on, or all the winter through
Upheld brave arms and with spring flowered anew
Above those living graves and graves of the dead;—
'Twas all such bitterness, but she nothing said.
She saw men as courageous boats that sailed
On all the seas, and some a far port hailed
Perhaps to sail again, or anchor there
Forever; some would quietly disappear
In stormless waters, and some in storms be broken
And all be hidden and no clear meaning spoken,
Nor any trace upon the waters linger.
Where the boat went the wind with hasty finger,
Savage and sly as aught of land could be,
Erased the little wrinkling of the sea.
O, in such enmity was man enisled,
Such loneliness, by foolish shades beguiled,
That it was bravery to see and live,
But cowardice to see and to forgive,
The wrong of evil, the wrong of death to life,
The defeat of innocence, the waste of strife,—
The heavy ills of time, injustice, pain—
In field and forest and flood rose huge and plain,
Brushing her mind with darkness, till she thought
Not with her brain, but all her nerves were wrought
Into an apprehension burning strong,

Unslackening, of mortality's old wrong.
But if her eyes she raised to those clear lonely
Altitudes of stars and ether only,
Her eyes fell and rebuked her as forbidden
With human mind to question what was hidden.
At summer dusk the broad moon rising high
Put gentleness in the vast strength of the sky,
Easing its weight; or the hot summer sun
Made noonday kind, and the hours lightly run.
But in those blazing midnights of the stars
Gathered and brightening for immortal wars
With spears and darts and arrows of sharp light,
She read the indifference of the infinite,
The high strife flashing through eternity
While on the earth stared mortals but as she.

O 'twas a living world that rose around
And in her sentience burned a hollow wound.
Such easy brightness as the poets see,
Or easy gloom, or hues of faerie,
She never saw, but into her own heart peered
To find what spirit indeed it was she feared:—
Whether in antique days a divine foe
Sprung branchlike from dense woods had wrought her woe;
Whether in antique days a pagan rite
(Herself a pagan still) unfilmed her sight
And taught her secrets never to be forgot,
And by man's generation pardoned not....
The same blood in ancestral veins ran fleet
As now made hers a road for pain's quick feet.
Into the marrow of her hidden life
Had poured the agony of their termless strife
With immaterial and material things;
And as a bird an unlearned music sings
Because a million generations sang,
So in her breast the old alarum rang,
So the old sorrowfulness in her thought
Renewed, and apprehensions all untaught;
As if indeed a creature primitive
Still did she in the world's dim morning live,
That wanted human warmth and gentleness
To make its solitude a little less.

Kindness gave solitude the lovely light
She loved, and made less terrible black midnight.
Even as a bird its unlearned music pours
Though windows all be blind and shut the doors,
And sings on still though no faint sound be heard

But wind and leaves and another lonely bird:
So poured she untaught kindness all around
And in that human music comfort found—
Music her own and music heard from others,
Prime music of all lovers, children, mothers,
Precarious music between all men sounding,
The horror of silent and dark Powers confounding.
Singing that music she could bravely live;
Hearing it, find less sorrow to forgive.

THE CANDLE

Time like a cloud
Has risen from the East
And whelmed the sky over
Even to the wide-arched West,
Darkening the blue,
Embrowning the early gold,
Until no more the eternal Sun
Looks simply through.

In each man's eyes
The cloud is set,
With but the chill light
Of silver January skies.
On each man's heart
Time's firm shadow falls,
And the mind throws but a candle's beam
On the dark walls.

But on those walls
Man paints his dream
Rejoicing purely
In the faithful candle's beam:
Lives by its beauty,
Pictures his heart's delight,
And with that only beam outbraves
Time's gathering night.

O spiritual flame,
Calm, faithful, bright!
Time may whelm over
All but this candle's light:
Shadow but shadow is;
Dark though it lies
'Tis blazon'd with man's long-dreamed dreams,

Pierced by his eyes.

OLD FIRES

The fire burns low
Where it has burned ages ago,
Sinks and sighs
As it has done to a hundred eyes
Staring, staring
At the last cold smokeless glow.

Here men sat
Lonely and watched the golden grate
Turn at length black;
Heard the cooling iron crack:
Shadows, shadows,
Watching the shadows come and go.

And still the hiss
I hear, the soft fire's sob and kiss,
And still it burns
And the bright gold to crimson turns,
Sinking, sinking,
And the fire shadows larger grow.

O dark-cheeked fire,
Wasting like spent heart's desire,
You that were gold,
And now crimson will soon be cold—
Cold, cold,
Like moon-shadows on new snow.

Shadows all,
They that watched your shadows fall.
But now they come
Rising around me, grave and dumb....
Shadows, shadows,
Come as the fire-shadows go.

And stay, stay,
Though all the fire sink cold as clay,
Whispering still,
Ancestral wise Familiars—till,
Staring, staring,
Dawn's wild fires through the casement glow.

THE CROWNS

Cherry and pear are white,
Their snows lie sprinkled on the land like light
On darkness shed.
Far off and near
The orchards toss their crowns of delight,
And the sun casts down
Another shining crown.

The wind tears and throws down
Petal by petal the crown
Of cherry and pear till the earth is white,
And all the brightness is shed
In the orchards far off and near,
That tossed by the road and under the green hill;
And the wind is fled.

Far, far off the wind
Has shaken down
A brightness that was as the brightness of cherry or pear
When the orchards shine in the sun.
—Oh there is no more fairness
Since this rareness,
The radiant blossom of English earth—is dead!

THE BRIGHT RIDER

All the night through I drank
Sleep like water or cool cider;
Life flowed over and I sank
Down below the night of clouds....
Then on a pale horse was rider
Through long brushing woods
Where the owl in silence broods,
Quavers, and is quiet again;
Where the grass dark and rank
Breathes on the still air its rain.
Rain and dark and green and sound
Closing slowly round
Swept me as I rode,
And rode on until I came
Where a white cold river flowed
Under woods thin and bare

In the moon's long candle flame.
Through the woods the wind crawled
Leviathan, and here and there
Branches creaked and old winds howled
Sick for home.
All the night I saw the river,
As a girl that sees beside her
Love, between fear and fear
Riding, and is dumb.
The white horse turned to cross the river,
But the waters like a wall
Rose and hung dark over all;
And as they fell the river wider
Wider grew, and sky was bare
Save of the sick candle's stare.
Death the divider
Glittered cold and dark and deep
Under banks of fear.
But that rider
Trembling, bright, rode on,
Trembling and bright rode on
Through green lanes of sleep.

TO THE HEAVENLY POWER

When this burning flesh
Burns down in Time's slow fire to a glowing ash;
When these lips have uttered
The last word, and the ears' last echoes fluttered;
And crumbled these firm bones
As in the chemic air soft blackened stones;
When all that was mortal made
Owns its mortality, proud yet afraid;

Then when I stumble in
The broad light, from this twilight weak and thin,
What of me will change,
What of that brightness will be new and strange?
Shall I indeed endure
New solitude in that high air and pure,
Aching for these fingers
On which my assurèd hand now shuts and lingers?

Now when I look back
On manhood's and on childhood's far-stretched track,
I see but a little child

In a green sunny world-home; there enisled
By another, cloudy world
Of unsailed waters all around him curled,
And he at home content
With the small sky of wonders over him bent:—

Lonely, yet not alone
Since all was friendly being all unknown;
To-day yesterday forgetting,
And never with to-morrow's sorrow fretting;
Not seeing good from ill
Since but to breathe and run and sleep was well;
Asking nor fearing nought
Since the body's nerves and veins held all his thought....

Such a child again shall I
Stray in some valley of infinity,
Where infinite finite seems
And nothing more immortal than my dreams?
Where earthly seasons play
Still with their snows and blossoms and night and day,
And no unsetting sun
Brightens the white cloud and awakes the moon?

In such half-life's half-light
To cloak with mortal an immortal sight?
With uninformed desire,
Shorn passion, gentle mind, contented fire,
Ignorant love; to run
But with the little journeys of the sun,
And at evening sleep
With birds and beasts, and stars rocked in the deep?

But maybe this man's mind
Will leave not its maturity behind,
And nothing will forget
Of all that teased or eased it here, while yet
A mortal dress it wore;
And these quick-darting thoughts and probings sore
More sharply then will turn;
And lonelier and yet hungrier the heart burn.

O, I would not forget
Earth is too rich, too dark, too sour, too sweet:—
Nor be divorcèd quite
From the late tingling of the nerves' delight.
Less I would never be
Than the deep-graving years have made of me—

A memory, pulse, mind,
Seed and harvest, a reaper and sower blind.

I shall no more be I
If I forget the world's joy and agony;
If I forget how strong
Is the assault of scarce-rebukèd wrong.
I shall no more be I
If my ears hear not earth's embittered cry
Perpetual; and forget
The unrighteous shackles on man's ankle set;

If no more my heart beat
Quicker because on earth is something sweet;
I shall no more be I
If the ancestral voices no more sigh
Familiar in my brain,
And leave me to cold silence and its pain,
And the bewildered stare
On an unhomely land in biting air:

If the blood no more vex
The heart with the importunities of sex,
If indeed marriage bind
No more body to body, mind to mind,
And love be powerless, cold,
That once by love's strength only was controlled,
And that chief spiritual force
Be dam'd back and stretch frozen to its source....

To the Heavenly Power I cry,
Foiled by these dreams of immortality,
"Let all be as Thou wilt,
And the foundations in Thy dark mind built;
Even infinity
Be but imagination's dream of Thee;
And let thought still, still
Vainly its waves on night's cliff break and spill.

"But, Heavenly Power," I'd cry,
Knowing how, near or far, He still is nigh,
"When this burning flesh
Is burnt away to a little driven ash,
What thing soever shall rise
From that cold ash unseen to unseen skies,
Grant that so much of me
Shall rise as may remember Thy world, and Thee."

SNOWS

Now the long-bearded chilly-fingered winter
Over the green fields sweeps his cloak and leaves
Its whiteness there. It caught on the wild trees,
Shook whiteness on the hedges and left bare
South-sloping corners and south-fronting smooth
Barks of tall beeches swaying 'neath their whiteness
So gently that the whiteness does not fall.
The ash copse shows all white between gray poles,
The oaks spread arms to catch the wandering snow.
But the yews—I wondered to see their dark all white,
To see the soft flakes fallen on those grave deeps,
Lying there, not burnt up by the yews' slow fire.
Could Time so whiten all the trembling senses,
The youth, the fairness, the all-challenging strength,
And load even Love's grave deeps with his barren snows?
Even so. And what remains?
The hills of thought
That shape Time's snows and melt them and lift up
Green and unchanging to the wandering stars.

THE THORN

The days of these two years like busy ants
Have gone, confused and happy and distressed,
Rich, yet sad with aching wants,
Crowded, yet lonely and unblessed.

I stare back as they vanish in a swarm,
Seeming how purposeless, how mean and vain,
Till creeping joy and brief alarm
Are gone and prick me not again.

The days are gone, yet still this heart of fire
Smouldering, smoulders on with ancient love;
And the red embers of desire
I would not, oh, nor dare remove!

Where is the bosom my head rested on,
The arms that caught my boy's head, the soft kiss?
Where is the light of your eyes gone?—
For now I know what darkness is....

It is the loneliness, the loneliness,
Since she that brought me here has left me here
With the sharp need of her to press
Sudden upon the nerve of fear;

It is the loneliness that wounds me still,
Shut from the generations that are past,
That with their blood my warm veins fill
And on my spirit their spirit cast;

That haunt me so and yet how strangely keep
Beyond communion, alone, alone,
Like that huge ancient hill asleep,
With to-day's noisy winds o'erblown.

There from the hill is sprung a single thorn,
Wind-twisted, straining from the earth to the skies,
Thin branches pleading with wild morn
And root that pressed in darkness lies.

From the unknown of earth and heaven are brought
Her strength, her weakness, death and bravest life;
Shadow and light and wind have wrought
Beauty from change, calm out of strife.

That tree upon the unchanging hill am I,
Alone upon the dark unwhispering hill:—
You in the stirless cold past lie,
But I ache warm and lonely still.

There's not a storm tossing among my boughs,
Nor gentle air drawn under quiet skies,
There's not an idle cloud that flows
Across the mind, nor bird that cries,

But says (if I have eyes, or ears to hear),
"You in this mortal being are alone."
And morn and noon and night-stars clear
Repeat, "Alone, alone, alone."

Yet the tree in wild storm her dark boughs shakes,
Thrusting her roots in the earth, her arms to heaven,
Fresh washed with dew when morning breaks;
And new light back to the light is given.

Is it that I that loved have yet forgot?
Is it that I that looked have yet been blind?

Longing, have yet remembered not
Nor heard you whispering in my mind?

But at a word you are nearer now than when
We sat and spoke, or merely looked and thought,
Knowing all speech superfluous then,
Since what we needed, silence brought;—

And your warm bosom my head rested on,
The arms that caught my boy's head, the soft kiss,
The brown grave eyes that gently shone—
Are here again, and brightness is.

Two years have gone, but nearer now are you,
Being dearer now; and this false loneliness
Is but a dream that cloudlike grew,
Then growing cloudlike less and less

Passes away, leaving me like the tree
Bright with the sun and wind and lingering dew;
Homely is all the world for me
Being sweeter with the sense of you.

CHANGE

Just as this wood, cast on the snaky fire,
Crushes the curling heads till smoke is thickened
And the ash sinks beneath the billet's weight,
And then again the hissing heads are quickened:
Just as this wood, by fretful fangs new stung,
Glows angrily, then whitens in the grate
And slowly smouldering smoulders away,
And dies defeated every famished tongue
And nothing's left but a memory of heat
And the sunk crimson telling warmth was sweet:
Just as this wood, once green with Spring's swift fire
Dies to a pinch of ashes cold and gray....
Just as this wood—

BEYOND THE BARN

I rose up with the sun
And climbed the hill.
I saw the white mists run

And shadows run
Down into hollow woods.

I went with the white clouds
That swept the hill.
A wind struck the low hedge trees
And clustering trees,
And rocked in each tall elm.

The long afternoon was calm
When down the hill
I came, and felt the air cool,
The shadows cool;
And I walked on footsore,

Saying, "But two hours more,
Then, the last hill....
Surely this road I know,
These hills I know,
All the unknown is known,

"And that barn, black and lone,
High on the hill—
There the long road ends,
The long day ends,
And travelling is over." ...

Nor thought nor travelling's over.
Here on the hill
The black barn is a shivering ruin,
A windy cold ruin.
I must go on and on,

Where often my thought has gone,
Up hill, down hill,
Beyond this ruin of Time;
Forgetting Time
I must follow my thought still.

LET HONOUR SPEAK

Let Honour speak, for only Honour can
End nobly what in nobleness began.
Nor hate nor anger may, though just their cause,
This strife prolong, if Honour whisper, Pause!
Let Honour speak.

For Honour keeps the ashes of the dead,
Accounts the anguish of all widowhead,
All childlessness, all sacrifice, defeat,
And all our dead have died for, though to live was sweet.
Let Honour speak,
Nor weariness nor weakness murmur, Stay!
Nor for this Now England's To be betray.
All else be dumb, for only Honour can
End nobly what in nobleness began.

TALK

So many were there talking that I heard
Nothing at first quite plain, as I sat down;
Until from this man's gibe and that keen word,
Another's chilly smile or peevish frown,
I caught their talk—but added none of mine.
They said how she still fumbled with her fate,
How she had banished visitants divine,
How long her sleep had been, her sloth how great,
How others had drawn near and passed her by,
While she luxuriously had dreamed, dreamed on,
She, she her own eternal enemy,
And wanting brain, brain, brain would be undone.
The glasses tinkled as they talked and laughed,
And if the door a moment hung ajar
The noises of the street, remotely soft,
Crept in as from a world sunken afar.
And still they talked, and then well pleased were pleased
To talk of other things—another's wife,
Money that ministers to a mind diseased,
And queer extravagant whims of death and life....
But I rose up, flushed at the careless slander,
Heedless what other laughing things were said,
And my bruised thoughts began to lift and wander
Far off, as from that jargoning I fled.
I saw the sharp green hills, the silver clouds
At rest upon the hills, the silver streams
Creeping between prone shoulders of dark woods.
I saw wide marshlands laved with level beams
Of the last light; I saw ships on the sea
That foamed hard by, stinging the fretful shore;
I smelt old ships on the deserted quay
That English sailors sailed, and will no more;
I thought of men I loved, and of dead men
I had longed to know—and each heroic ghost

Rose and moved on, and left me alone again
Aching for love and splendour glimpsed and lost.

God knows what things I thought when anger broke
Her narrow dam and swept my spirit clean.
Yet I for very shame not a word spoke,
But to my heart's heart caught the things I had seen,
And England, England! murmuring, stood and stared,
Swept like a lover with sweet influence
In brain and bone—and happy that I had spared
Her nobleness the indignity of defence.

THE UNDYING

In thin clear light unshadowed shapes go by
Small on green fields beneath the hueless sky.
They do not stay for question, do not hear
Any old human speech: their tongue and ear
Seem only thought, for when I spoke they stirred not
And their bright minds conversing my ear heard not.
—Until I slept or, musing, on a heap
Of warm crisp fern lay between sense and sleep
Drowsy, still clinging to a strand of thought
Spider-like frail and all unconscious wrought.
For thinking of that unforgettable thing,
The war, that spreads a loud and shaggy wing
On things most peaceful, simple, happy and bright,
Until the spirit is blind though the eye is light;
Thinking of all that evil, envy, hate,
The cruelty most dark, most desolate;
Thinking of the English dead—"How can you dead,"
I muttered, "with your life and young joy shed,
How can you but in these new lands of life
Relume the fiery passion of old strife—
Just anger, mortal hate, the natural scorn
Of men true-born for all things foully born?"
For I had thought that not death's touch could still
In man's clean spirit the hate of good for ill.

But now to see their shapes go lightly by
On those vast fields, clear 'neath the hueless sky,
With not one furious gesture, and (when seen
With but the broad dark hedgerow space between)
No eye's disdain, no thin drawn face of grief,
But pondering calm or lightened look and brief
Smile almost gay;—yet all seen in the air

That driv'n mist makes unreal everywhere—
"So strange," I breathed, "How can you English dead
Forget them for whose life your life was shed?"

It was no voice that answered, yet plain word
Less plain is than the unspoken that I heard,
As I lay there on the dry heap of fern
And watched them pass, mix, disappear and return,
And felt their mute speech into empty senses burn:
"Earth's is the strife. The Heavenly Powers that sent
The gray globe spinning in the firmament,
The Heavenly Powers that soon or late will stay
The spinning, as a child that tires of play,
And globe by spent globe put forgot away
In some vast airless hollow: could they see
Or seeing endure immortal misery
Made out of mortal, and undying hate
Earth's perishing agonies perpetuate?
O spirits unhappy, if from earth men brought
The mind's disease, the sickness of mad thought!
Sooner the Heavenly Powers would let them lie
Eternally unrising 'neath a sky
Arctic and lonely, where death's starven wind
Raged full-delighted:—sooner would those kind
Serenities man's generation cast
Back into nothingness, than heaven should waste
With finite anguish infinitely prolonged
Until the Eternal Spring were stained and wronged.
O, even the Heavenly Powers at such a breath
From mortal shores would fade and fade to death."

—Was it a voice or but a thought I heard,
Mine or another's, in my boughs that stirred
Waking the leafy darkness of the mind?
Was it a voice, or but a new-roused wind
That answered—"O, I know, I know, I know!
The oldest rivers into the full sea flow
And there are lost: so everything is lost,
On midnight waves into oblivion tost.
Yet—the high passion, the pity, the joy and pride,
The righteousness for which these men have died,
The courage, the uncounted sacrifice,
The love and beauty, all that's beyond all price;
That this, the immortal heart of mortal man,
Should be—O tell me what, tell me again, again—
Petals lost on the river of the years
When April sweetness pauses, fades and disappears!
That this high Quarrel should be quenched in death

As some vexed petty plaint unworthy breath;
That the blood and the tears should never rise
Renewed, accusing in grave judgment skies ...
Tell me again—O, rather tell me not
Lest that ill telling never be forgot."

And then I rose from that warm ferny heap
And my thoughts climbed from the abyss of sleep.
No more in human guise did cloud-shapes pass,
Nor sighed with sad intelligence the grass.
I saw the hueless sky break into blue,
And I remembered how that heaven I knew
When, a small child, I gazed at the great height,
And thought of nothing but the blue and white,
Pools of sweet blue swimming in fields of light.
And as tired men from mine and stithy turn
While still the midnight fires unslackened burn
Flushing their road, and so reach home and then
Dream of old childhood's days and dream again;
So I forgot those inward fires and found
Old happiness like dew lying all around.
Under the hedge I stood and far below
Saw on the Worcester Plain the swift clouds flow
Like ships on seas no greener than the Plain
That shone between October sun and rain;
And thinking how time's plenteousness would bring
Back and more bright the young delicious Spring,
Between wet brambles thrust my hand, and tasted
Ripe berries on neglected boughs that wasted.

THE NATIVE COUNTRY

Where is that country? The unresting mind
Like a lapwing nears and leaves it and returns.
I know those unknown hill-springs where they rise,
I know the answer of the elms to the wind
When the wind on their heaving bosom lies
And sleeps. I know the grouping pines that crown
The long green hill and fling their darkness down,
A never-dying shadow; and well I know
How in the late months the whole wide woodland burns
Unsmoking, and the earth hangs still as still.
I know the town, the hamlets and the lone
Shelterless cottage where the wind's least tone
Is magnified, and his far-flung thundering shout
Brings near the incredible end of the world. I know!

Even in sleep-walk I should linger about
Those lanes, those streets sure-footed, and by the unfenced stream go,
Hearing the swift waters past the locked mill flow.
Where is that country? It lies in my mind,
Its trees and grassy shape and white-gashed hill
And springs and wind and weather; its village stone
And solitary stone are in my mind;
And every thought familiarly returns
To find its home, and birdlike circling still
Above the smouldering beeches of November
And the bare elms and rattled hedgerows of December.
That native country lies deep in my mind
For every thought and true affection's home.
And like that mental land are you become,
Part of that land, and I the thought that turns
Towards home. And as in that familiar land I find
Myself among each tree, spring, road and hill,
And at each present step my past footsteps remember;
So you in all my inward being lies,
In you my history, my earth and stream and skies.
Your late fire is it that in my boughs yet burns,
Your stone that to my passing footfall cries.

PART III

STONE TREES

Last night a sword-light in the sky
Flashed a swift terror on the dark.
In that sharp light the fields did lie
Naked and stone-like; each tree stood
Like a tranced woman, bound and stark.
Far off the wood
With darkness ridged the riven dark.

And cows astonished stared with fear,
And sheep crept to the knees of cows,
And conies to their burrows slid,
And rooks were still in rigid boughs,
And all things else were still or hid.
From all the wood
Came but the owl's hoot, ghostly, clear.

In that cold trance the earth was held
It seemed an age, or time was nought.
Sure never from that stone-like field

Sprang golden corn, nor from those chill
Gray granite trees was music wrought.
In all the wood
Even the tall poplar hung stone still.

It seemed an age, or time was none ...
Slowly the earth heaved out of sleep
And shivered, and the trees of stone
Bent and sighed in the gusty wind,
And rain swept as birds flocking sweep.
Far off the wood
Rolled the slow thunders on the wind.

From all the wood came no brave bird,
No song broke through the close-fall'n night,
Nor any sound from cowering herd:
Only a dog's long lonely howl
When from the window poured pale light.
And from the wood
The hoot came ghostly of the owl.

IT WAS THE LOVELY MOON

It was the lovely moon—she lifted
Slowly her white brow among
Bronze cloud-waves that ebbed and drifted
Faintly, faintlier afar.
Calm she looked, yet pale with wonder,
Sweet in unwonted thoughtfulness,
Watching the earth that dwindled under
Faintly, faintlier afar.
It was the lovely moon that lovelike
Hovered over the wandering, tired
Earth, her bosom gray and dovelike,
Hovering beautiful as a dove....
The lovely moon:—her soft light falling
Lightly on roof and poplar and pine—
Tree to tree whispering and calling,
Wonderful in the silvery shine
Of the round, lovely, thoughtful moon.

THE HOUNDS

Far off a lonely hound

Telling his loneliness all round
To the dark woods, dark hills, and darker sea;

And, answering, the sound
Of that yet lonelier sea-hound
Telling his loneliness to the solitary stars.

Hearing, the kennelled hound
Some neighbourhood and comfort found,
And slept beneath the comfortless high stars.

But that wild sea-hound
Unkennelled, called all night all round—
The unneighboured and uncomforted cold sea.

HECTOR

Sleep, sleep, you great and dim trees, sleeping on
The still warm, tender cheek of night,
And with her cloudy hair

Brushed: sleep, for the violent wind is gone;
Only remains soft easeful light,
And shadow everywhere,

And few pale stars. Hardly has eve begun
Dreaming of day renewed and bright
With beams than day's more fair;

Scarce the full circle of the day is run,
Nor the yellow moon to her full height
Risen through the misty air.

But from the increasing shadowiness is spun
A shadowy shape growing clear to sight,
And fading. Was it Hector there,

Great-helmed, severe?—and as the last sun shone
Seeming in solemn splendour dight
Such as dream heroes bear;

And such his shape as heroes stare upon
In sleep's tumultuary fight
When a cry's heard, "Beware!" ...

—'Twas Hector, but the moment-splendour's gone:

Shadow fast deepens into night,
Night spreads—cold, wide, bare.

LISTENING

There is a place of grass
With daisies like white pools,
Or shining islands in a sea
Of brightening waves.

Swallows, darting, brush
The waves of gentle green,
As though a wide still lake it were,
Not living grass.

Evening draws over all,
Grass and flowers and sky,
And one rich bird prolongs the sweet
Of day on the edge of dark.

The grass is dim, the stars
Lean down the height of heaven;
And the trees, listening in all their leaves,
Scarce-breathing stand.

Nothing is as it was:
The bird on the bough sings on;
The night, pure from the cloud of day,
Is listening.

STONES

Small yellow stones
That, lifted, through my idle fingers fall
Leaving a score—
And these I toss between the parted lips
Of the lapping sea,
And the sea tosses again with millions more—
Yellow and white stones;
Then drawing back her snaky long waves all,
Leaves the stones
Yellow and white upon the sandy shore....
As they were bones
Yellow and white left on the silent shore

Of an unfoaming far unvisioned Sea.

THE ENEMIES

The angry wind
That cursed at me
Was nothing but an evil sprite
Vexed with any man's delight.

And strange it seemed
That a dark wind
Should run down from a mountain steep
And shout as though the world were asleep.

But when he ceased
And silence was—
Who could but fear what evil sprite
Crept through the tunnels of the night?

THE SILVERY ONE

Clear from the deep sky pours the moon
Her silver on the heavy dark;
The small stars blink.

Against the moon the maple bough
Flutters distinct her leafy spears;
All sound falls weak....

Weak the train's whistle, the dog's bark,
Slow steps; and rustling into her nest
At last, the thrush.

All's still; only earth turns and breathes.
Then that amazing trembling note
Cleaves the deep wave

Of silence. Shivers even that silvery one;
Sigh all the trees, even the cedar dark
——O joy, and I.

THE FLUTE

It was a night of smell and dew
When very old things seemed how new;
When speech was softest in the still
Air that loitered down the hill;
When the lime's sweetness could but creep
Like music to slow ears of sleep;
When far below the lapping sea
Lisped but of tired tranquillity....
No, 'twas a night that seemed almost
Of real night the little ghost,
As though a painter painted it
Out of the shallows of his wit—
The easy air, the whispered trees,
Faint prattle of strait distant seas,
Pettiness all: but hark, hark!
Large and rich in the narrow dark
Music rose. Was music never
Braver in her pure endeavour
Against the meanness of the world.
Her purple banner she unfurled
Of stars and suns upon the night
Amazed with the strange living light.
The notes rose where the dark trees knelt;
Their fiery joy made stillness melt
As flame in woods the low boughs burns,
Sere leaves, dry bushes, flame-shaped ferns.
The notes rose as great birds that rise
Majestically in lofty skies,
And in white clouds are lost; and then
Briefly they hushed, and woke again
Renewed.
Slowly silence came
As smoke after sinking flame
That spreads and thins across the sky
When day pales before it die.

STARS

The naked stars, deep beyond deep,
Burn purely through the nervèd night.
Over the narrow sleep
Of men tired of light;

Deep within deep, as clouds behind
Huge grey clouds hidden gleaming rise,

Untroubled by sharp wind
In cold desert skies.

Cold deserts now with infinite host
Of gathered spears at watch o'er small
Armies of men lost
In glooms funereal.

O bitter light, all-threatening stars,
O tired ghosts of men that sleep
After stern mortal wars
'Neath skies chill and steep.

These mortal hills, this flickering sea,
This shadowy and thoughtful night,
Throb with infinity,
Burn with immortal light.

TEN O'CLOCK AND FOUR O'CLOCK

It stands there
Tall and solitary on the edge
Of the last hill, green on the green hill.
Ten o'clock the tree's called, no one knows why.
Perhaps it was planted there at ten o'clock
Or someone was hanged there at ten o'clock—
A hundred such good reasons might be found,
But no one knows. It vexed me that none knew,
Seeing it miles and miles off and then nearer
And nearer yet until, beneath the hill,
I looked up, up, and saw it nodding there,
A single tree upon the sharp-edged hill,
Holding its leaves though in the orchard all
Leaves and fruit were stripped or hung but few
Red and yellow over the littered grass.
—It vexed me, the brave tree and senseless name,
As I went through the valley looking up
And then looked round on elm and beech and chestnut
And all that lingering flame amid the hedge
That marked the miles and miles.
Then I forgot:
For through the apple-orchard's shadow I saw
Between the dark boughs of the cherry-orchard
A great slow fire which Time had lit to burn
The mortal seasons up, and leave bare black
Unchanging Winter.

Weston-sub-Edge.

THE YEW

The moon gave no light.
The clouds rode slowly over, broad and white,
From the soft south west.
The wind, that cannot rest,
Soothed and then waked the darkness of the yew
Until the tree was restless too.

Of all the winds I knew
I thought, and how they muttered in the yew,
Or raved under the eaves,
Or nosed the fallen dry leaves,
Or with harsh voice holloa'd the orchard round,
With snapped limbs littering the ground.

And I thought how the yew
Between the window and the west his shadow threw,
Grave and immense,
Darkening the dark past thought and sense,
And how the moon would make the darkness heavenly bright:
But the moon gave no light.

NOVEMBER SKIES

Than these November skies
Is no sky lovelier. The clouds are deep;
Into their gray the subtle spies
Of colour creep,
Changing that high austerity to delight,
Till even the leaden interfolds are bright.
And, where the cloud breaks, faint far azure peers
Ere a thin flushing cloud again
Shuts up that loveliness, or shares.
The huge great clouds move slowly, gently, as
Reluctant the quick sun should shine in vain,
Holding in bright caprice their rain.
And when of colours none,
Not rose, nor amber, nor the scarce late green,
Is truly seen,—
In all the myriad gray,

In silver height and dusky deep, remain
The loveliest,
Faint purple flushes of the unvanquished sun.

DELIGHT

Winter is fallen
On the wretched grass,
Dark winds have stolen
All the colour that was.
No leaf shivers:
The bare boughs bend and creak as the wind moans by
Fled is the fitful gleam of brightness
From the stooping sky.

A robin scatters
Like bright rain his song,
Of merry matters
The sparrows gossip long.
Snow in the sky
Lingers, soon to cover the world with white,
And hush the slender enchanting music
And chill the delight.

But snow new fallen
On the stiffened grass
Gives back beauty stolen
By the winds as they pass:—
Turns the climbing hedge
Into a gleaming ladder of frozen light:
And hark, in the cold enchanted silence
A cry of delight!

CHANGE

A late and lonely figure stains the snow,
Into the thickening darkness dims and dies.
Heavily homeward now the last rooks go,
And dull-eyed stars stare from the skies.
A whimpering wind
Sounds, then's still and whimpers again.

Yet 'twas a morn of oh, such air and light!
The early sun ran laughing over the snow,

The laden trees held out their arms all white
And whiteness shook on the white below.
Lovely the shadows were,
Deep purple niches, 'neath a dome of light.

And now night's fall'n, the west wind begins to creep
Among the stiff trees, over the frozen snow;
An hour—and the world stirs that was asleep,
A trickle of water's heard, stealthy and slow,
First faintly here and there,
And then continual everywhere.

And morn will look astonished for the snow,
And the warm, wind will laugh, "It's gone, gone, gone!"—
And will, when the immortal soft airs blow,
This mortal face of things change and be gone
So—and with none to hear
How in the night the wind crept near?

SLEEPING SEA

The sea
Was even as a little child that sleeps
And keeps
All night its great unconsciousness of day.
No spray
Flashed when the wave rose, drooped, and slowly drew away.
No sound
From all that slumbering, full-bosomed water came;
The sea
Lay mute in childlike sleep, the moon was a gold candle-flame.
No sound
Save when a faint and mothlike air fluttered around.
No sound:
But as a child that dreams and in his full sleep cries,
So turned the sleeping sea and heaved her bosom of slow sighs.

THE WEAVER OF MAGIC

Weave cunningly the web
Of twilight, O thou subtle-fingered Eve!
And at the slow day's ebb
With small blue stars the purple curtain weave.
If any wind there be,

Bid it but breathe lightly as woodland violets o'er the sea;
If any moon, be it no more than a white fluttering feather.
Call the last birds together.

O Eve, and let no wisp
Of day's distraction thine enchantment mar;
Thy soft spell lisp
And lure the sweetness down of each blue star.
Then let that low moan be
A while more easeful, trembling remote and strange, far oversea;
So shall the easeless heart of love rest then, or only sigh,
Hearing the swallows cry!

THE DARKSOME NIGHTINGALE

Why dost thou, darksome Nightingale,
Sing so distractingly—and here?
Dawn's preludings prick my ear,
Faint light is creeping up the vale,
While on these dead thy rarer
Song falls, dark night-farer.

Were it not better thou shouldst sing
Where the drenched lilac droops her plume,
Spreading frail banners of perfume?
Or where the easeless pines enring
The river-lullèd village
Whose lads the lilac pillage?

Oh, if aught songful these hid bones
Might reach, like the slow subtle rain,
Surely the dead had risen again
And listened, white by the white stones;
Back to rich life song-charmed,
By ghostly joys alarmed.

This may not be. And yet, oh still
Pour like night dew thy richer speech
Some late-lost youth perchance to reach,
Or unloved girl; and stir and fill
Their passionless cold bosoms
Under red wallflower blossoms!

UNDER THE LINDEN BRANCHES

Under the linden branches
They sit and whisper;
Hardly a quiver
Of leaves, hardly a lisp or
Sigh in the air.
Under the linden branches
They sit, and shiver
At the slow air's fingers
Drawn through the linden branches
Where the year's sweet lingers;
And sudden avalanches
Of memories, fears,
Shake from the linden branches
Upon them sitting
With hardly a sigh or a whisper
Or quiver of tears.

STRIFE

The wind fought with the angry trees.
All morning in immense unease
They wrestled, and ruin strawed the ground,
And the north sky frowned.
The oak and aspen arms were held
Defiant, but the death was knelled
Of slender saplings, snappy boughs,
Twigs brittle as men's vows.
How moaned the trees the struggle through!
Anger almost to madness grew.
The aspen screamed, and came a roar
Of the great wind locked in anguish sore,
Desolate with defeat ... and then
Quiet fell again:
The trees slept quiet as great cows
That lie at noon under broad boughs.
How pure, how strange the calm; but hist!...
Was it the trees by the wind kissed?
Or from afar, where the wind's hid,
A throb, a sob?

FOREBODING

O linger late, poor yellow whispering leaves!
As yet the eves
Are golden and the simple moon looks through
The clouds and you.
O linger yet although the night be blind,
And in the wind
You wake and lisp and shiver at the stir
And sigh of her
Whose rimy fingers chill you each and all:
And so you fall
As dead as hopes or dreams or whispered vows....
O then the boughs
That bore your busy multitude shall feel
The cold light steal
Between them, and the timorous child shall start,
Hearing his heart
Drubbing affrighted at the frail gates, for lo,
The ghostly glow
Of the wild moon, caught in the barren arms
Of leafless branches loud with night's alarms!

DISCOVERY

Beauty walked over the hills and made them bright.
She in the long fresh grass scattered her rains
Sparkling and glittering like a host of stars,
But not like stars cold, severe, terrible.
Hers was the laughter of the wind that leaped
Arm-full of shadows, flinging them far and wide.
Hers the bright light within the quick green
Of every new leaf on the oldest tree.
It was her swimming made the river run
Shining as the sun;
Her voice, escaped from winter's chill and dark,
Singing in the incessant lark....
All this was hers—yet all this had not been
Except 'twas seen.
It was my eyes, Beauty, that made thee bright;
My ears that heard, the blood leaping in my veins,
The vehemence of transfiguring thought—
Not lights and shadows, birds, grasses and rains—
That made thy wonders wonderful.
For it has been, Beauty, that I have seen thee,
Tedious as a painted cloth at a bad play,
Empty of meaning and so of all delight.
Now thou hast blessed me with a great pure bliss,

Shaking thy rainy light all over the earth,
And I have paid thee with my thankfulness.

MORE THAN SWEET

The noisy fire,
The drumming wind,
The creaking trees,
And all that hum
Of summer air
And all the long inquietude
Of breaking seas—

Sweet and delightful are
In loneliness.
But more than these
The quiet light
From the morn's sun
And night's astonished moon,
Falling gently upon breaking seas.

Such quietness
Another beauty is—
Ah, and those stars
So gravely still
More than light, than beauty pour
Upon the strangeness
Of the heart's breaking seas.

THE BRIGHTNESS

Away, away—
Through that strange void and vast
Brimmed with dying day;
Away,
So that I feel
Only the wind
Of the world's swift-rolling wheel.

See what a maze
Of whirling rays!
The sharp wind
Weakens; the air
Is but thin air,

Not fume and flying fire....
O, heart's desire,
Now thou art still
And the air chill.

And but a stem
Of clear cold light
Shines in this stony dark.
Farewell, world of sense,
Too fair, too fair
To be so false!
Hence, hence
Rosy memories,
Delight of ears, hands, eyes.
Rise
When I bid, O thou
Tide of the dark,
Whelming the pale last,
Reflection of that vast
Too-fair deceit.

Ah, sweet
To miss the vexing heat
Of the heart's desire:
Only to know
All's lost, lost....
Sweet
To know the lack of sweet.

—Thou fool!
See how the steady dark
Is filled with eyes—
Eyes that smile,
Hot, then how cool!
Eyes that were stars till thou
Mad'st them eyes.
O, the tormenting
Look, the unrelenting
Passionate kiss
Of their wild light on thine—
Light of thine eyes!

As if one could
Loathe the world for too much sweetness!
All the air's a flame,
Wonderful—yet the same
Thou'st hated,
Being briefly sated

With sweet of sweetness.

Forgive a heart whose madness
Was not of madness born,
But of mere wild
Waste of desire....
Who does not know
One speaks so, or so,
Out of mere passion
That sees not love
From hate, nor life from death,
Nor hell from heaven?

In the East—oh, that flashed
Brightness, past
The loveliness even
Of sunset's flush!

THE HOLY MOUNTAINS

The holy mountains,
The gay streams,
Heavy shadows,
And tall, trembling trees;
The light that sleeps
Between the heavy shadows,
Wind that creeps
Faintly, from far-off seas—

The mountains' light,
Waters' noise,
Trees' shadows,
Clear, slow, calm air,
Are dreams, dreams,
And far, far-fallen echoes
Of secret worlds
And inconceivable dark seas.

RAPTURE

If thou hast grief
And passion vex the spirit that is in thee—

There was a stony beach

Where the heat flickered and the little waves
Whispered each to each.
Dove-coloured was that stony beach,
And white birds hungering hovered over
The shining waves;
And men had kindled there
A great fierce heap of golden flame—
Spoiled grasses with dead buttercups and pale clover.
The agonising flame
Yearned in its vitals towards the quiet air
And died in a little smoke.
And on the coloured beach the black warm ash
Remained.

Then on that warm ash
Another heap of grasses was outpoured,
And instant came
Another knot of struggling yellow smoke
That burst into new agonies of flame,
Dying into a drift of smoke;
And on the coloured beach the black cold ash
Remained.

Or is thy grief too deep,
Passion too dear, the spirit in thee asleep?—

Twelve deep and sombre, still,
Expectant, hushed,
The miles-long crowd stood—and then listening.
The nervous drums,
The unendurable, low reeds:
Silence—and then the nearing drums
Again, again the thrilling reeds,
And then
(The deep crowd hushed)
Following an almightier King
That rode unseen,
Drew near the tributary magnificence....
Hushed, hushed,
The deep crowd stood, devouring, listening;
But a child on his father's shoulder cried,
"Hurrah, hurrah!"—

Only have thou no fear
Pride, but no fear.

MUSIC COMES

Music comes
Sweetly from the trembling string
When wizard fingers sweep
Dreamily, half asleep;
When through remembering reeds
Ancient airs and murmurs creep,
Oboe oboe following,
Flute answering clear high flute,
Voices, voices—falling mute,
And the jarring drums.

At night I heard
First a waking bird
Out of the quiet darkness sing....
Music comes
Strangely to the brain asleep!
And I heard
Soft, wizard fingers sweep
Music from the trembling string,
And through remembering reeds
Ancient airs and murmurs creep;
Oboe oboe following,
Flute calling clear high flute,
Voices faint, falling mute,
And low jarring drums;
Then all those airs
Sweetly jangled—newly strange,
Rich with change....
Was it the wind in the reeds?
Did the wind range
Over the trembling string;
Into flute and oboe pouring
Solemn music; sinking, soaring
Low to high,
Up and down the sky?
Was it the wind jarring
Drowsy far-off drums?

Strangely to the brain asleep
Music comes.

THE IDIOT

He stands on the kerb

Watching the street.
He's always watching there,
Listening to the beat
Of time in the street,
Listening to the thronging feet,
Laughing at the world that goes
Scowling or laughing by.

He sees Time go by,
An old lonely man,
Crooked and furtive and slow.
He laughs as he sees
Time shambling by
While he stands at his ease,
Until Time smiles wanly back
At his laughing eye.

Greed's great paunch,
Lean Envy's ill looks,
Fond forgetful Love,
He reads them like books:
Whatever their tongue
He reads them like children's books,
Stands staring and laughing there
As all they go by.

O, he laughs as he sees
The fat and the thin,
The simple, the solemn and wise
Nod-nodding by.
He stares in their eyes,
Till they're angry and murmur, Poor fool!
And he hears and he laughs again
From the depth of his folly.

Even when with heavy
Plume and pall
The sleeky coaches roll by,
Coffin, flowers and all,
He laughs, for he sees
Crouched on the coffin a small
Yellowy shape go by—
Death, uneasy and melancholy.

THE MOUSE

Standing close by you
In the cold light
Of two tall candles
That measure the dark of night,
I hear the mouse,
The only thing that's moving
In the quiet house.

Don't you hear it,
That furious mouse?
How can you sleep so deep
And that noise in the house?
Won't you stir
At the furious scratching
In the cupboard there?

No! a sharper sound
Would wake you not;
Not the sweetest fluting
Tease you back to thought.
Yet the scratching mouse
Makes all my flesh a nervous
Haunted house.

O, the dream, the dream
Must be sweet and deep
If life's scratching's heard not
On your cold sleep.
Yet if you should hear it,
So furious and fretful—
How could you bear it?

HAPPINESS

I have found happiness who looked not for it.
There was a green fresh hedge,
And willows by the river side,
And whistling sedge.

The heaviness I felt was all around.
No joy sang in the wind.
Only dull slow life everywhere,
And in my mind.

Then from the sedge a bird cried; and all changed.
Heaviness turned to mirth:

The willows the stream's cheek caressed,
The sun the earth.

What was it in the bird's song worked such change?
The grass was wonderful.
I did not dream such beauty was
In things so dull.

What was it in the bird's song gave the water
That living, sentient look?
Lent the rare brightness to the hedge?
That sweetness shook

Down on the green path by the running water?
Or the small daisies lit
With light of the white northern stars
In dark skies set?

What was it made the whole world marvellous?
Mere common things were joys.
The cloud running upon the grass,
Children's faint noise,

The trees that grow straight up and stretch wide arms,
The snow heaped in the skies,
The light falling so simply on all;
My lifted eyes

That all this startling aching beauty saw?
I felt the sharp excess
Of joy like the strong sun at noon—
Insupportable bliss!

COMFORTABLE LIGHT

Most comfortable Light,
Light of the small lamp burning up the night,
With dawn enleagued against the beaten dark;
Pure golden perfect spark;

Or sudden wind-bright flame,
That but the strong-handed wind can urge or tame;
Chill loveliest light the kneeling clouds between,
Silverly serene;

Comfort of happy light,

That mouse-like leaps amid brown leaves, cheating sight;
Clear naked stars, burning with swift intense
Earthward intelligence;—

Sensitive, single
Points in the dark inane that purely tingle
With eager fire, pouring night's circles through
Their living blue;

Dark light still waters hold;
Broad silver moonpath trodden into gold:
Candle-flame glittering through the traveller's night—
Most comfortable light....

And lovelier, the eye
Where light from darkness shines unfathomably,
Light secret, clear, shallow, profound, known, strange,
Constant alone in change:—

Not that wild light that turns
Hunted from dying eyes when the last fire burns;
O, not that bitter light of wounded things,
When bony anguish springs

Sudden, intolerable;
Nor light of mad eyes gleaming up from hell....
Come not again, wild light! Shine not again,
Hill-flare of pain!

But thou, most holy light....
Not the noon blaze that stings, too fiercely bright,
Not that unwinking stare of shameless day;
But thou, the gray,

Nun-like and silent, still,
Fine-breathed on many an eastern bare green hill;
Keen light of gray eyes, cool rain, and stern spears;
Sad light, but not to tears:—

—O, comfort thou of eyes
Watching expectant from chill northern skies,
Excellent joy for lids heavy with night—
Strange with delight!

"Hallo, hallo!" impatiently he cried,
And I replied,
Sleepily, "Hallo—hallo!"
No sound then; and I stretched
My hand for the receiver, all my nerves
Tingling and listening.
My hand clutched nothing, and I lit
The candle—strange!
I could have sworn it was the shouting wire....
But no!
Besides, a bare and unfamiliar room
And he, why, long-forgotten, maybe dead.
Yet all around,
Filling the silence up with tiny sound,
A million tremulous thin echoings,
"Hallo—hallo—
Hallo!"

FEAR

There was a child that screamed,
And if it was the gathering tingling dark,
Or if it was the tingling silences
Between few words,
Or if the water's drip and quivering drip—
Who knows?
Or if the child half sleeping suddenly dreamed—

Who knows? for she knew not, but was afraid,
And then angry with fear,
And then it seemed afraid of all the voices
Echoing hers.
And then afraid again of that drip, drip
Of water somewhere near.

Yet a man dying would not with such fear
Scream out at hell.
Easier it were to die than to endure,
Unless death brought the instant consciousness
Of all the wrongs of all lost years
Falling like water, drip after trembling drip
Upon the naked anguish of the soul.

But death's stupidity
Is gentle to the lunatic last wits.
Little of terror, little of consciousness,

But stupor, a great ease,
Narrowing silences,
And silence;
And then no more the drip, drip of the years,
No more the strangeness, agonies and fears;
No more the noise, but one imponderable unhaunted
Hush....

I heard the child that cried
Chattering a moment after in the light,
And singing out of such contentment as
Lamps and familiar voices bring.
She needs must sing
Now that sharp, spiny agony thrust no more,
Nor water fell, drip, drip by quivering drip;
Her face was bright,
Unapprehensive as a day in spring.

WAKING

Lying beneath a hundred seas of sleep
With all those heavy waves flowing over me,
And I unconscious of the rolling night
Until, slowly, from deep to lesser deep
Risen, I felt the wandering seas no longer cover me
But only air and light....

It was a sleep
So dark and so bewilderingly deep
That only death's were deeper or completer,
And none when I awoke stranger or sweeter.
Awake, the strangeness still hung over me
As I with far-strayed senses stared at the light.

I—and who was I?
Saw—oh, with what unaccustomed eye!
The room was strange and everything was strange
Like a strange room entered by wild moonlight;
And yet familiar as the light swept over me
And I rose from the night.

Strange—yet stranger I.
And as one climbs from water up to land
Fumbling for weedy steps with foot and hand,
So I for yesterdays whereon to climb
To this remote and new-struck isle of time.

But I found not myself nor yesterday—

Until, slowly, from deep to lesser deep
Risen, I felt the seas no longer over me
But only air and light.
Yes, like one clutching at a ring I heard
The household noises as they stirred,
And holding fast I wondered. What were they?

I felt a strange hand lying at my side,
Limp and cool. I touched it and knew it mine.
A murmur, and I remembered how the wind died
In the near aspens. Then
Strange things were no more strange.
I travelled among common thoughts again;

And felt the new forged links of that strong chain
That binds me to myself, and this to-day
To yesterday. I heard it rattling near
With a no more astonished ear.
And I had lost the strangeness of that sleep,
No more the long night rolled its great seas over me.

—O, too anxious I!
For in this press of things familiar
I have lost all that clung
Round me awaking of strangeness and such sweetness
Nothing now is strange
Except the man that woke and then was I.

THE FALL

From that warm height and pure,
The peak undreamed of out of heavy air
Rising to heaven more strange and rare;
From that amazed brief sojourn, exquisite, insecure;

Fallen from thence to this,
From all immortal sunk to mortal sweet,
To slow gross joys from joy so fleet,
Fallen to mere remembrance of unsustainable bliss....

O harsh, O heavy air,
Difficult endurance, pain of common things!
The slow sun east to westward swings,
The flat-faced moon climbs labouring with a senseless stare.

From that inconceivable height——
O inward eyes that saw and ears that heard,
Spiritual swift wings that stirred
In that warm-flushing air and unendurable light;

When I was as mere down
On a swift-running youthful wind uptaken
Over tall trees, white mountains, shaken,
Into the uttermost azure lifted, lifted alone.

From that peak can it be
That I am fallen, fallen that was so high?
Or was that truly, surely I?
Who is it crawls here now, sad, uncontentedly?

Fallen from that high content,
—Fool, thou that wast content merely with bliss!
Happy those lovers that will not kiss;
Never to be fulfilled was the heart's endless passion meant.

Never on joys attainable
To linger, never on easy near delight—
O bitter, unreached infinite,
Merciful defeat, availless anguish, hunger unendurable!

O who shall be in longing wise,
Skilled in refusal, in embracing free,
Glad with earth's innocent ecstasy,
Yet all the uncomprehended heaven in his eyes!

STAY

Stay, thou desired one, stay!
Brighten the curious darkness of the world.
Cold through the chill dark swings the sleeping world,
Sense-heavy, dreaming dully of clear day.
No moon, no stars, no sound of wind or seas:
Wearily sleeping in immense unease,
Dreams, dreams the world of day.
Stay, thou adored one, stay,
Who on the dark hang'st lamps of gold delight,
Gold flames amid the purple pit of night.
Stay, stay,
Who the cool dawn's most lovely gray
Mak'st lovelier with rose of far away.

Stay, thou, who buildest wonder of things mean
(More truly so they're seen).
Stay—nay, fly not, nay—stay;
Youth gone, remain thou yet and yet.
Though the world spin in darkness and forget
The light,
Stay thou, whose coming's joy and flight despair.
Thou unimaginably more than fair,
Brief unsustainable strange dream, stay yet!
Lamping the world's close unsustainable dark
With golden unimaginable day.

SHADOWS

The shadow of the lantern on the wall,
The lantern hanging from the twisted beam,
The eye that sees the lantern, shadow and all.

The crackle of the sinking fire in the grate,
The far train, the slow echo in the coombe,
The ear that hears fire, train and echo and all.

The loveliness that is the secret shape
Of once-seen, sweet and oft-dreamed loveliness,
The brain that builds shape, memory, dream and all....

A white moon stares Time's thinning fabric through,
And makes substantial insubstantial seem,
And shapes immortal mortal as a dream;
And eye and brain flicker as shadows do
Restlessly dancing on a cloudy wall.

WALKING AT EVE

Walking at eve I met a little child
Running beside a tragic-featured dame,
Who checked his blitheness with a quick "For shame!"
And seemed by sharp caprice froward and mild.
Scarce heeding her the sweet one ran, beguiled
By the lit street, and his eyes too aflame;
Only, at whiles, into his eyes there came
Bewilderment and grief with terror wild.

So, Beauty, dost thou run with tragic life;

So, with the curious world's caress enchanted,
Even of ill things thine ecstasy dost make;
Yet at the touch of fear and vital strife
The splendours thy young innocency forsake,
And with thy foster-mother's woe thou art haunted.

THE PHYSICIAN

She comes when I am grieving and doth say,
"Child, here is that shall drive your grief away."
When I am hopeless, kisses me and stirs
My breast with the strong lively courage of hers.
Proud—she will humble me with but a word,
Or with mild mockery at my folly gird;
Fickle—she holds me with her loyal eyes;
Remorseful—tells of neighbouring Paradise;
Envious—"Be not so mad, so mad," she saith,
"Envied and envier both race with Death"
She my good Angel is: and who is she?—
The soul's divine Physician, Memory.

VISION AND ECHO

I have seen that which sweeter is
Than happy dreams come true.
I have heard that which echo is
Of speech past all I ever knew.
Vision and echo, come again,
Nor let me grieve in easeless pain!

It was a hill I saw, that rose
Like smoke over the street,
Whose greening rampires were upreared
Suddenly almost at my feet;
And tall trees nodded tremblingly
Making the plain day visionary.

But ah, the song, the song I heard
And grieve to hear no more!
It was not angel-voice, nor child's
Singing alone and happy, nor
Note of the wise prophetic thrush
As lonely in the leafless bush.

It was not these, and yet I knew
That song; but now, alas,
My unpurged ears prove all too gross
To keep the nameless air that was
And is not; and my eyes forget
The vision that I follow yet.

Yet though forgetful I did see.
And heard, but cannot tell,
And on my forehead felt an air
Unearthly, on my heart a spell.
I have seen that which deathless is,
And heard—what I for ever miss!

REVISITATION

It is here—the lime-tree in the garden path,
The lilac by the wall, the ivied wall
That was so high, the heavy, close-leaved creeper,
The harsh gate jarring on its hinges still,
The echoing clean flags—all
The same, the same, and never more the same.

That mound was once a hill,
The old lime-tree a forest (now as small
As the poor lilac by the ivied wall),
And this neglected narrow greenery
A wilderness, and I its king and keeper;
Lying upon the grass I saw the sky
And all its clouds: the garden edged the sky.

The harsh gate jars upon its hinges still.

UNPARDONED

Gentle as the air that kisses
The splendid and ignoble with one breath,
Gentle as obliterating Death—
Though you be gentler yet,
In days when the old, old things begin to fret
The backward-looking consciousness,
Will you forget?
Or if remembering, will you forgive?

But there is one severer.
Stung by your forgivingness so great
Shall I forgive you then?—
Basest of men
Would rise in bitterness and sting again.
Not if you should forget
Could I forget:
Or if remembering, myself could I forgive?

Never! And yet such things have been,
And ills as dark forgiven or forgot.
But in those black hours when the heart burns hot
And there's no nerve that's not
Quick with the sense of things unheard, unseen—
A terrible voice that's mine yet not mine cries,
"Can that Eternal Righteousness
Remembering forgive?"

SOME HURT THING

I came to you quietly when you were lying
In perfect midnight sleep.
Your dark soft hair was all about your pillow,
So black upon the white.
I could not see your face except the lovely
Curve of the pale cheek;
Your head was bent as though your stirless slumber
Was sea-like heavy and deep.
The wind came gently in at the wide window,
Shaking the candle-light
And shadows on the wall; and there was silence,
Or sound but far and weak.
By the bedside your daytime toys were gathered:
The bright bell-ringing wheel,
Dolls clad in violent yellow and vermilion,
Strings of gay-coloured beads....
But you were far and far from these beside you,
Entranced with other joys
In fresh fields, among other children running:
Your voice, I knew, must peal
Purely among their high unearthly voices
Over green daisied meads,
While I stood watching your scarce-heaving slumber
Beside your human toys—
And heard, faint from the woods all through the night,
The cry of some hurt thing that moaned for light.

THE WAITS

Frost in the air and music in the air,
And the singing is sweet in the street.
She wakes from a dream to a dream—O hark!
The singing so faint in the dark.

The musicians come and stand at the door,
A fiddler and singers three,
And one with a bright lamp thrusts at the dark,
And the music comes sudden—O hark!

She hears the singing as sweet as a dream
And the fiddle that climbs to the sky,
With head 'neath the curtain she stares out—O hark!
The music so strange in the dark.

She listens and looks and sees but the sky,
While the fiddle is sweet in the porch,
And she sings back into the singing dark
Hark, herald angels, hark!

IN THE LANE

The birds return,
The blossom brightens again the cherry bough.
The hedges are green again
In the airless lane,
And hedge and blossom and bird call, Now, now, now!

O birds, return!
Who will care if the blossom die on the bough,
Or the hedge be bare again
In the screaming lane?
For what they were these are not, are not now.

The one gone makes
All that remain seem strange and lonely now.
She will not walk here again
In the blossoming lane:—
And there's a dead bough in every blossoming bough.

THE LAST TIME

For the last time,
The last, last time,
The last ...
All those last times have I lived through again,
And every "last" renews itself in pain—
Yes, each returns, and each returns in vain:
You return not, the last remains the last,
And I remain to cast
Weak anchors of my love in shifting sands
Of faith:—
The anchors drag, nothing I see save death.

Together we
Talked and were glad. I could not see
That one black gesture menaced you and me!
We kissed, and parted;
I left you, and was even merry-hearted....
And now my love is thwarted
That reaches back to you and searches round,
And dares not look on that harsh turfless mound.

And that last time
We walked together and the air acold
Hummed shrill around; the time that you
Walked heavily,
And I dared not to see,
Nor dared you then to speak of what must be.
We knew not what the shut days would unfold—
Nay, could not know till all the days were told....
But that last time we walked together, and
—And walk no more together, nor clasp hand
In hand, just stiffly as we used to do.

Never in dreams,
O happy, never in stealing dreams
We meet; never again
I live by night the day's slow-dying pain ...
The last, last time,
The last—
That time is past; yet in too-golden day
My heart goes from me whispering,
"Where are you—you—you—you?"
And comes back easeless to an easeless breast.
But at night I rest
Dreamless as derelict ships ride out to sea

Empty, and no bird even on the snapp'd mast
Pauses: into oblivion her shadow's cast;
Into the empty night goes lonely she,
And into sleep go—oh, more lonely I.

YOU THAT WERE

You that were
Half my life ere life was mine;
You that on my shape the sign
Set of yours;
You that my young lips did kiss
When your kiss summed up my bliss....
Ah, once more
You to kiss were all my bliss!

You whom I
Could forget—strange, could forget
Even for days (ah, now the fret
Of my grief!);
You who loved me though forgot;
Welcomed still, reproaching not....
Ah, that now
That forgetting were forgot!

You that now
On my shoulder as I go
Put your hand that wounds me so;
You that brush
Yet my lips with that one last
Kiss that bitters all things past....
How shall I
Yet endure that kiss the last?

You that are
Where the feet of my blind grief
Find you not, nor find relief;
You that are
Where my thought flying after you
Broken falls and flies anew,
Now you're gone
My love accusing aches for you.

March 4, 1911.

"THE LIGHT THAT NEVER WAS ON SEA OR LAND"

O gone are now those eager great glad days of days, but I remember
Yet even yet the light that turned the saddest of sad hours to mirth;
I remember how elate I swung upon the thrusting bowsprits,
And how the sun in setting burned and made the earth all unlike earth.

O gone are now those mighty ships I haunted days and days together,
And gone the mighty men that sang as crawled the tall craft out to sea;
And fallen ev'n the forest tips and changed the eyes that watched their
burning,
But still I hear that shout and clang, and still the old spell stirs in
me.

And as to some poor ship close locked in water dense and dark and vile
The wind comes garrulous from afar and sets the idle masts a-quiver;
And ev'n to her so foully docked, swift as the sun's first beam at dawn
The sea-bird comes and like a star wheels by and down along the river; —

So to me the full wind blows from far strange waters echoingly,
And faint forgotten longings break the fast-sealed pools within my
breast;
So to me when sunset glows the scream comes of the white sea-bird,
And all those ancient raptures wake and wakes again the old unrest.

I see again the masts that crowd and part lie trees in living wind,
I hear again the shouts and cries and lip-lap of the waveless pool;
I see again the smalling cloud of sail that into distance fades,
I am again the boy whose eyes with tears of grief and hope are full.

AT EVENING'S HUSH

Now pipe no more, glad Shepherd,
Your joys from this fair hill
Through golden eves and still:
There sounds from yon dense quarry
A burden harsh and sorry.

No piping now, poor Shepherd.
Men strive with violent hand,
And anger stirs the bland
Blithe heaven that ne'er yet trembled,
Save with great spirits assembled.

No more, no more, sad Shepherd,

Let thy bright fingers stray
Idly in the old way;
No more their nimble glancing
Set gleeful spirits a-dancing.

Put by thy pipe, O Shepherd!
There needs no note of thine
For men deaf, undivine....
And lest brute hands should take it,
O sorrowful Shepherd, break it!

HAPPY DEATH

Bugle and battle-cry are still,
The long strife's over;
Low o'er the corpse-encumbered hill
The sad stars hover.

It is in vain, O stars! you look
On these forsaken:
Awhile with blows on blows they shook,
Or struck unshaken.

Needs now no pity of God or man ...
Tears for the living!
They have 'scaped the confines of life's plan
That holds us grieving.

The unperturbed soft moon, the stars,
The breeze that lingers,
Wake not to ineffectual wars
Their hearts and fingers.

Warriors o'ercoming and o'ercome,
Alike contented,
Have marched now to the last far drum,
Praised, unlamented.

Bugle and battle-cry are still,
The long strife's over;
Oh, that with them I had fought my fill
And found like cover!

WISDOM AND A MOTHER

Why, mourner, do you mourn, nor see
The heavenly Earth's felicity?

I mourn for him, my Dearest, lost,
Who lived a frail life at my cost.

A grief like yours how many have known!

Were that a balm to ease my own!
Or rather might I not accuse
The Hand that does not even choose,
But, taking blindly, took my best,
And as indifferently takes the rest ...
Like mine? Is there denied to me
Even Sorrow's singularity?

THE THRUSH SINGS

Singeth the Thrush, forgetting she is dead....
How could you, Thrush, forget that she is dead?
Or though forgetting, sing—and she is dead?
O hush,
Untimely, truant Thrush!

Singeth the Thrush, "I sing that she is dead!"
Thou thoughtless Thrush, she loved you who is dead,
Singeth the Thrush, "I sing her praise though dead."
O hush,
Untimely, grievous Thrush!

Singeth the Thrush, "I sing your happy dead,
I sing her who is living, and no more dead,
I sing her joy—she is no longer dead."
O hush,
Enough, thou heavenly Thrush!

TO MY MOTHER

No foreign tribute from a stranger-hand,
Mother, I bring thee, whom not Heaven's songs
Would as an alien reach.... Ah, but how far
From Heaven's least heavenly is the changing note
And changing fancy of these fitful cries!

Mother, forgive them, as the best of me
Has ever pleaded only for thy pardon,
Not for thy praise.
Mother, there is a love
Men give to wives and children, lovers, friends;
There is a love which some men give to God.
Ah! between this, I think, and that last love,
Last and too-late-discovered love of God,
There shines—and nearer to the love of God—
The love a man gives only to his mother,
Whose travail of dear thought has never end
Until the End. Oh that my mouth had words
Comfortable as thy kisses to the boy
Who loved while he forgot thee! Now I love,
Sundered and far, with daily heart's remembrance
The face the wind brings to me, the sun lights,
The birds and waters sing; the face of thee
Whom I love with a love like love of God.

THE UNUTTERED

For so long and so long had I forgot,
Serenely busied
With thousand things; at whiles desire grew hot
And my soul dizzied
With hapless and insatiable salt thirst.
Nor was I humbled
Saving with shame that, running with the worst
My feet yet stumbled.
Pride and delight of life enchained my heart,
My heart enchanted,
And oh, soft subtle fingers had their part,
And eyes love-haunted.
But while my busy mind was thus intent,
Or thus surrendered,
What was it, oh what strange thing was it sent
Through all that hindered
A thrill that woke the buried soul in me?—
It seemed there fluttered
A thought—or was it a sudden fear?—of Thee,
Remote, unuttered.

FAIR EVE

Fair Eve, as fair and still
As fairest thought, climbs the high sheltering hill;
As still and fair
As the white cloud asleep in the deep air.

As cool, as fair and cool,
As starlight swimming in a lonely pool;
Subtle and mild
As through her eyes the soul looks of a child.

A linnet sings and sings,
A shrill swift cleaves the air with blackest wings;
White twinkle-tails
Run frankly in their meadow as day fails.

On such a night, a night
That seems but the full sleep of tired light,
I look and wait
For what I know not, looking long and late.

Is it for a dream I look,
A vision from the Tree of Heaven shook,
As sweetness shaken
From the fresh limes on lonely ways forsaken?

A dream of one, maybe,
Who comes like sudden wind from oversea?
Or most loved swallow
Whom all fair days and golden musics follow?—

More sudden yet, more strange
Than magic airs on magic hills that range:—
Of one who'll steep
The soul in soft forgetfulness ere it sleep.

Yes, down the hillside road,
Where Eve's unhasty feet so gently trod,
Follow His feet
Whose leaf-like echoes make even spring more sweet.

THE SNARE

Loose me and let me go!
I am not yours.
I do not know
Your dark name ev'n, O Powers

That out of the deep rise
And wave your arms
To weave strange charms.

Though the snare of eyes
You weave for me,
As a pool lies
In wait for the moon when she
Out of the deep will rise;
And though you set
Like mist your net;

And though my feet you catch,
O dark, strange Powers,
You may not snatch
My soul, or call it yours.
Out of your snare I rise
And pass your charms,
Nor feel your harms.

You loose me and I go:
O see the arms
Spread for me! lo,
His lips break your charms.
From the deep did He rise
And round me set
His Love for net.

O HIDE ME IN THY LOVE

O hide me in Thy love, secure
From this earth-clinging meanness.
Lave my uncleanness
In Thy compassionating love!

Bury this treachery as deep
As mercy is enrooted.
My days ill-fruited
Shake till the shrivelled burden fall.

Put by those righteous arrows, Lord,
Put even Thy justice by Thee;
So I come nigh Thee
As came the Magdalen to Thy feet.

And like a heavy stone that's cast

In a pool, on Thee I throw me,
And feel o'erflow me
Ripples of pity, deep waves of love.

PRAYER TO MY LORD

If ever Thou didst love me, love me now,
When round me beat the flattering vans of life,
Kissing with rapid breath my lifted brow.
Love me, if ever, when the murmur of strife,
In each dark byway of my being creeps,
When pity and pride, passion and passion's loss
Wash wavelike round the world's eternal cross,
Till 'mid my fears a new-born love indignant leaps.

If ever Thou canst love me, love me yet,
When sweet, impetuous loves within me stir
And the frail portals of my spirit fret—
The love of love, that makes Heaven heavenlier,
The love of earth, of birds, children and light,
Love of this bitter, lovely native land....
O, love me when sick with all these I stand
And Death's far-rumoured wings beat on the lonely night.

THE TREE

Oh, like a tree
Let me grow up to Thee!
And like a Tree
Send down my roots to Thee.

Let my leaves stir
In each sigh of the air,
My branches be
Lively and glad in Thee;

Each leaf a prayer,
And green fire everywhere ...
And all from Thee
The sap within the Tree.

And let Thy rain
Fall—or as joy or pain
So that I be

Yet unforgot of Thee.

Then shall I sing
The new song of Thy Spring,
Every leaf of me
Whispering Love in Thee!

EARTH TO EARTH

What is the soul? Is it the wind
Among the branches of the mind?
Is it the sea against Time's shore
Breaking and broken evermore?
Is it the shore that breaks Time's sea,
The verge of vast Eternity?
And in the night is it the soul
Sleep needs must hush, must needs kiss whole?
Or does the soul, secure from sleep,
Safe its bright sanctities yet keep?
And oh, before the body's death
Shall the confined soul ne'er gain breath,
But ever to this serpent flesh
Subdue its alien self afresh?
Is it a bird that shuns earth's night,
Or makes with song earth's darkness bright?
Is it indeed a thought of God,
Or merest clod-fellow to clod?
A thought of God, and yet subdued
To any passion's apish mood?
Itself a God—and yet, O God,
As like to earth as clod to clod?

ON A PIECE OF SILVER

So! the fierce acid licks the silver clean,
Unwonted plain the superscription's seen
Round the cleared head; the metal, virgin-bright,
Shines a mild Moon to the Sun candle-light.
And in these floating stains, this evil murk,
All your change-crowded, moment-histories lurk,
Voluble Silverling! Dost yield me now
Your chance-illumined record, and allow
Prying of idle eyes?... you came a boon
To men as weary as any the weak moon

Shines on but cheers not; you were life in death;
Almost a God to give the prize of breath,
Almost a God to give the prize of joy,
Almost a God—but God! the veriest toy
Child's fingers break, from death to buy back life,
Turn the keen trouble of grief's eager knife,
Or sense-confounded hearts heal of the ancient strife.
O Coin that men have toiled for, lacked and mourned,
Sold life for and sold honour, won and scorned;
O Coin that oft hast been a spinning Fate,
Yet impotent her bitterness to abate;
O Coin that Love contemns, reckoning nought
(But with you, ah, Love's best is sold and bought)—
Heart of the harlot, you; the Judas blood
Hell's devils leech on; you the Price of God!

THE ESCAPE

Like one who runs
Fearful at night, he knows not why,
Dreading the loneliness, yet shuns
The highway's casual company;

Wherefore he hastes,
The friendly gloom of ancient trees
Unheeding, and the shining wastes
Lying broad and quiet as the seas;

The beauty of night
Hating for very fear, until
Beyond the bend a lowly light
Beams single from a lowly sill;

And the poor fool,
Flying the sacred, solemn dark,
Leaves gladly the large, cool
Night for that serviceable spark;

And thankful then
To have 'scaped the peril of the way,
Turns not his timid steps again
That night, but waits the common day;—

So I, as weak,
Have fled the great hills of Thy love,
Too faint to hear what Thou dost speak,

Too feeble with fear to look above,

And hasten to win
Some flickering, brief security,
In sinful sleep or waking sin,
From the enfolding thought of Thee!

WONDER

Following upon the faint wind's fickle courses
A feather drifts and strays.
My thought after her thought
Floated—how many ways and days!

She swayed me as the wind swayeth a feather.
I was a leaf upon
Her breath, a dream within
Her dream. The dream how soon was done!

For now all's changed, not Time's change more wondrous,
I am her sun, and she
(Herself doth swear) the moon;
Or she the ship upon my sea.

How should this be? I know not; I so grossly
Mastering her spirit pure.
O, how can her bird's breast
My nervous and harsh hand endure?

Tell me if this be love indeed, fond lovers,
That high stoop to low,
Soul be to flesh subdued;
That the sun around the earth should go?

I know not: I but know that love is misery,
O'erfilled with delight.
Day follows night: her love
Is gay as day, yet strange as night.

LAMBOURN TOWN

The rain beat on me as I walked,
In the roadside it ran and muttered.
It seemed the rain to the wind talked

Of storm: in the wind the wild cloud fluttered.

Across the down, now bleak and loud,
I went and the rain ran with me.
How swift the rain, how low the cloud!
No heavenly comfort could I see,

Nor comfort of low beaming light
From any casement creeping out.
The swift rain on the patient night
Swept, and anon would great winds shout.

Rain, rain, nought else, until I turned
The thrusting shoulder of the down,
And through the mist of rain there burned
The few green lanterns of the town.

And in the rain the night was lit
With my love's eyes burning for me;
Her white face in the dark was sweet,
Her hands like moonflowers quiveringly

Fell upon mine, and each was dashed
With rain blown in from streaming eaves,
While overhead the broad flood plashed
Noisily on the broad plane leaves.

Within we heard the gurgle-glock
In the pipe, the tip-tap on the sill
Like the same ticking of the clock;
We heard the water-butt o'erspill,

The wind come blustering at the door,
The whipped white lilac thrash the wall;
The candle flame upon the floor
Crept between shadows magical....

In the black east a pallid ray
Rose high; and sweeping o'er the down
The slow increase of stormless day
Lit the wet roofs of Lambourn town.

THE LAMP

The lamp shone golden where she slept,
Shining against deep-folded shadows.

There was no stir but her slow breathing
Save when a long sigh crept
Between her lips.

Her hair spread dark in that faint light,
Her shut eyes showed the long dark lashes—
Still now, that with her laughter quivered.
On the white sheet lay white
And limp her hands.

Golden against the shadow shone
The lamp's small flame, till dawn was brightening,
And on the flame a gold beam slanted.
The shadows lingering on
Grew faint and thin.

Sleeping she murmured, stirred and sighed,
A dream from her sleep-vision faded.
Her earthly eyes 'neath languid eyelids
Wakened: her bosom cried,
"Come back, come back,

"Come back, my dream!" Rising she drest
Her beauty's lamp with cunning fingers.
She had the look of birds a-flutter
Round dewy trees with breast
Throbbing with song.

WHO IS IT THAT ANSWERS?

The clouds no more are flocking
After the flushing sun;
Bees end their long droning,
The bat's hunt is begun;
And the tired wind that went flittering
Up and down the hill
Lies like a shadow still,
Like a shadow still.

Who is it that's calling
Out of the deepening dark,
Calling, calling, calling?—
No!—yet hark!
The sleepy wind wakes, carrying
Up and down the hill
A voice how small and still,

How sweet and still!

Who is it that answers
Out of a quiet cloud—
"Stay, oh stay! I come, I come!"
Cried at last aloud?
My voice, my heart went answering
Up and down the hill—
Mine so strange and still,
Mine grave and still.

WAITING

Rich in the waning light she sat
While the fierce rain on the window spat.
The yellow lamp-glow lit her face,
Shadows cloaked the narrow place
She sat adream in. Then she'd look
Idly upon an idle book;
Anon would rise and musing peer
Out at the misty street and drear;
Or with her loosened dark hair play,
Hiding her fingers' snow away;
And, singing softly, would sing on
When the desire of song had gone.
"O lingering day!" her bosom sighed,
"O laggard Time!" each motion cried.
Last she took the lamp and stood
Rich in its flood,
And looked and looked again at what
Her longing fingers' zeal had wrought;
And turning then did nothing say,
Hiding her thoughts away.

ABSENCE

Distance no grace can lend you, but for me
Distance yet magnifies your mystery.
With you, and soon content, I ask how should
In your two eyes be hid my heaven of good?
How should your own mere voice the strange words speak
That tease me with the sense of what's to seek
In all the world beside? How your brown hair,
That simply and neglectfully you wear,

Bind my wild thoughts in its abundant snare?
With you, I wonder how you're stranger than
Another woman to another man;
But parted—and you're as a ship unknown
That to poor castaways at dawn is shown
As strange as dawn, so strange they fear a trick
Of eyes long-vexed and hope with falseness sick.
Parted, and like the riddle of a dream,
Dark with rich promise, does your beauty seem.
I wonder at your patience, stirless peace,
Your subtle pride, mute pity's quick release.
Then are you strange to me and sweet as light
Or dew; as strange and dark as starless night.
Then let this restless parting be forgiven:
I go from you to find in you strange heaven.

SLEEP

Not a dream brush your sleep,
Not a thought wake and creep
In upon your spirit's slumber;
Not a memory encumber,
Nor a thievish care unbar
Sleep's portcullis that no star
Nor sentry hath. I'll not speak
With my soul even: no, nor seek
Other happiness for you
When you this happy sleep sleep through.
Let no least desire waver
Between us, nor impatience quaver;
No sudden nearness of me flush
Your veins with welcome.... Hush, hush!
Be still, my thoughts, lest you creep
Unawares into her sleep.

YOUR SHADOW

From Swindon out to White Horse Hill
I walked, in morning rain,
And saw your shadow lying there.
As clear and plain
As lies the White Horse on the Hill
I saw your shadow lying there.

Over the wide green downs and bleak,
Unthinking, free I walked,
And saw your shadow fluttering by.
Almost it talked,
Answering what I dared not speak
While thoughts of you ran fluttering by....

So on to Baydon sauntered, teased
With that pure native air.
Sometimes the sweetness of wild thyme
The strings of care
Did pluck; sometimes my soul was eased
With more than sweetness of wild thyme.

Sometimes within a pool I caught
Your face, upturned to mine.
And where sits Chilton by the waters
Your look did shine
Wildly in the mill foam that sought
To hide you in those angry waters.

And yet, O Sweet, you never knew
Those downs, the thymy air
That with your spirit haunted is—
Yes, everywhere!
Ah, but my heart is full of you,
And with your shadow haunted is.

THE FULL TIDE

Now speaks the wave, whispering me of you;
In all his murmur your music murmurs too.
O 'tis your voice, my love, whispering in
The wave's voice, even your voice so far and thin;
And mine to yours answering clear is heard
In the high lonely voice of the last bird.

And when, my love, the full tide runneth again,
Shall yet the seabird call, call, call in vain?
Will not the tide wake in my heart and stir
The old rich happiness that's sunken there?
Thou moon of love, bid the retreated tide
Return, for which the wandering bird has cried.

HANDS

Your hands, your hands,
Fall upon mine as waves upon the sands.
O, soft as moonlight on the evening rose,
That but to moonlight will its sweet unclose,
Your hands, your hands,
Fall upon mine, and my hands open as
That evening primrose opens when the hot hours pass.

Your hands, your hands,
They are like towers that in far southern lands
Look at pale dawn over gloom-valley'd miles,
White temple towers that gleam through mist at whiles.
Your hands, your hands,
With the south wind fall kissing on my brow,
And all past joy and future is summed in this great "Now!"

THE NIGHT WATCH

Beneath the trees with heedful step and slow
At night I go,
Fearful upon their whispering to break
Lest they awake
Out of those dreams of heavenly light that fill
Their branches still
With a soft murmur of memoried ecstasy.
There 'neath each tree
Nightlong a spirit watches, and I feel
His breath unseal
The fast-shut thoughts and longings of tired day,
That flutter away
Mothlike on luminous soft wings and frail
And moonlike pale.
There in the flowering chestnuts' bowering gloom
And limes' perfume
Wandering wavelike through the moondrawn night
That heaves toward light,
There hang I my dark thoughts and deeper prayers;
And as the airs
Of star-kissed dawn come stirring and o'er-creep
The ford of sleep,
Thy shape, great Love, grows shadowy in the East,
Thine accents least
Of all those warring voices of false morn:
And oh, forlorn

Thy hope, thy courage vanishing, thine eyes
Sad with surprise.
Oh, with the dawn I know, I know how vain
Is love that's fain
To beat and beat against her obstinate door.
For as once more
It groans, she passes out not heeding me,
Nay, will not see:—
As when a man, rich and of high estate,
Sees at his gate
(Or will not see) a famishing poor wretch,
Whose longings fetch
Old anger from his pain-imprisoning breast,
Till sad despair his anger puts to rest.

THE HAUNTED SHADOW

Fair Trees, O keep from chattering so
When I with my more fair do go
Beneath your branches;
For if I laugh with her your sigh
Her rare and sudden mirth puts by,
Or your too noisy glee will take
Persuasion from my lips and make
Her deaf as winter.

O be not as the pines—that keep
The shadow-charmèd light asleep—
Perverse and sombre!
For when we in the pinewood walked
And of young love and far age talked,
Their solemn haunted shadow broke
Her peace—ah, how the sharp sob shook
Her shadowed bosom!

ALONE AND COLD

Do not, O do not use me
As you have used others.
Better you did refuse me:
You have refused others.
Better, far better hope to banish
A small child than, grown old,
Hope should decay, his vigour vanish,

And I be left alone and
Cold, cold.

Ah, use no guile nor cunning
If you should even yet love me.
Hark, Time with Love is running,
Death cloud-like floats above me.
Love me with such simplicity
As children, frankly bold,
Do love with; oh, never pity me,
Though I be left alone and
Cold, cold.

INEVITABLE CHANGE

Young as the Spring seemed life when she
Came from her silent East to me;
Unquiet as Autumn was my breast
When she declined into her West.

Such tender, such untroubling things
She taught me, daughter of all Springs;
Such dusty deathly lore I learned
When her last embers redly burned.

How should it hap (Love, canst thou say?)
Such end should be to so pure day?
Such shining chastity give place
To this annulling grave's disgrace?

Such hopes be quenched in this despair,
Grace chilled to granite everywhere?
How should—in vain I cry—how should
That be, alas, which only could!

LONELINESS

How green and strange the light is,
Creeping through the window.
Lying alone in bed,
How strange the night is!

How still and chill the air is.
It seems no sound could live

Here in my room
That now so bare is.

All bright and still the room is,
But easeless here am I.
Deep in my heart
Cold lonely gloom is!

I HEARD A VOICE UPON THE WINDOW BEAT

I heard a voice upon the window beat
And then grow dim, grow still.
Opening I saw the snowy sill
Marked with the robin's feet.
Chill was the air and chill
The thoughts that in my bosom beat.

I thought of all that wide and hopeless snow
Crusting the frozen lands.
Of small birds that in famished bands
A-chill and silent grow.
And how Earth's myriad hands
Clutched only hills of frosted snow.

And then I thought of Love that beat and cried
Famishing at my breast;
How I, by chilling care distrest,
Denied him, and Love died....
O, with what sore unrest
Love's ghost woke with the bird that cried!

FIRST LOVE

I

"No, no! Leave me not in this dark hour,"
She cried. And I,
"Thou foolish dear, but call not dark this hour;
What night doth lour?"
And nought did she reply,
But in her eye
The clamorous trouble spoke, and then was still.

O that I heard her once more speak,

Or even with troubled eye
Teach me her fear, that I might seek
Poppies for misery.
The hour was dark, although I knew it not,
But when the livid dawn broke then I knew,
How while I slept the dense night through
Treachery's worm her fainting fealty slew.

O that I heard her once more speak
As then—so weak—
"No, no! Leave me not in this dark hour."
That I might answer her,
"Love, be at rest, for nothing now shall stir
Thy heart, but my heart beating there."

II

Come back, come back—ah, never more to leave me!
Come back, even though your constant longing grieve me,
Longing for other looks and hands than mine.
By all that's most divine
In your frank human beauty, come and cover
With that deceiving smile the love your lover
Has taught you, and the light that in your eyes
Tells of the painful joys that make your ruinous Paradise.

Come back, that so, upon the shining meadow
When the sun draws the magic of your shadow,
Or when the red fire's gradual sinking light
Yields up the room to night;
Seeing you thus or thus I may recapture
The very sharpness of remembered rapture:—
So it may seem, by exquisite deceit,
You are yet mine, I yours, and life yet rare and sweet.

Come back—no, come not back now, come back never;
That day you went I knew it was for ever.
I know you, how the spectre of cold shame
Would chill you if you came.
Lo, here first love's first memory abideth;
Here in my heart the image of you yet hideth.
But though you should come back and hope thrilled me anew,
First love would yet be dead—oh, it would not be you!

III

O but what grace if I could but forget you!
You have made league with all familiar things—

The thrush that still, evening and morning, sings,
The aspen leaves that sigh
"My dear!" with your true voice when I pass by....
O, and that too-long-dying flush of tender sky
That minds me, and with sense too grave for tears,
Of those forever dead too-blissful years.

Yet 'twere a miracle could I forget you,
Since even dead things, once sensible of you,
Yield up your ghost; as all the garden through
Murmurs the rose, "'Twas she
Shook in her palm the dew that shone in me;"
And on the stairs your recent footstep echoingly
Sounds yet again, and each dark doorway speaks
Of you toward whom my sharpened longing seeks.

O that I could forget or not regret you!
Could I but see you as I have seen a fair
Child under apple-burdened boughs that bear
Morn's autumn beauty, and
Seeing her saw all heaven at my hand,
And all day long that happy child before me stand....
Not thus I see you, but as one drowning sees
Home, friends—and loves his very enemies!

THE CALL

Is it the wind that stirs the trees,
Is it the trees that scratch the wall,
Is it the wall that shakes and mutters,
Is it a dumb ghost's call?

The wind steals in and twirls the candle,
The branches heave and brush the wall,
But more than tree or wild wind mutters
This night, this night of all.

"Open!" a cry sounds, and I gasp.
"Open!" and hands beat door and wall.
"Open!" and each dark echo mutters.
I rise, a shape and shadow tall.

"Open!" Across the room I falter,
And near the door crouch by the wall;
Thrice bolt the door as the voice mutters
"Open!" and frail strokes fall.

"Open!" The light's out, and I shrink
Quaking and blind against the wall;
"Open!" no sound is, yet it mutters
Within me now, this night of all.

Was it the wind that stirred the trees,
Was it the trees that scratched the wall,
Was it the wall that shook and muttered.
Or Love's last, ghostly call?

THE SHADE

I saw him as he went
With merry voice and eye.

I met him when he came
Back, tired but the same—
The same clear voice, bright eye,
Merry laugh, quick reply.

And now, if I but look
Unnoting at a book,
Or from the window stare
At dark woods newly bare,
I see that shining eye,
The same as when he went:

—But whose is the low sigh,
The cold shade o'er me bent?

HAPPY IS ENGLAND NOW

There is not anything more wonderful
Than a great people moving towards the deep
Of an unguessed and unfeared future; nor
Is aught so dear of all held dear before
As the new passion stirring in their veins
When the destroying Dragon wakes from sleep.

Happy is England now, as never yet!
And though the sorrows of the slow days fret
Her faithfullest children, grief itself is proud.
Ev'n the warm beauty of this spring and summer

That turns to bitterness turns then to gladness
Since for this England the beloved ones died.

Happy is England in the brave that die
For wrongs not hers and wrongs so sternly hers;
Happy in those that give, give, and endure
The pain that never the new years may cure;
Happy in all her dark woods, green fields, towns,
Her hills and rivers and her chafing sea.

Whate'er was dear before is dearer now.
There's not a bird singing upon his bough
But sings the sweeter in our English ears:
There's not a nobleness of heart, hand, brain
But shines the purer; happiest is England now
In those that fight, and watch with pride and tears.

THE STARS IN THEIR COURSES

And now, while the dark vast earth shakes and rocks
In this wild dream-like snare of mortal shocks,
How look (I muse) those cold and solitary stars
On these magnificent, cruel wars?—
Venus, that brushes with her shining lips
(Surely!) the wakeful edge of the world and mocks
With hers its all ungentle wantonness?—
Or the large moon (pricked by the spars of ships
Creeping and creeping in their restlessness),
The moon pouring strange light on things more strange,
Looks she unheedfully on seas and lands
Trembling with change and fear of counterchange?

O, not earth trembles, but the stars, the stars!
The sky is shaken and the cool air is quivering.
I cannot look up to the crowded height
And see the fair stars trembling in their light,
For thinking of the starlike spirits of men
Crowding the earth and with great passion quivering:—
Stars quenched in anger and hate, stars sick with pity.
I cannot look up to the naked skies
Because a sorrow on dark midnight lies,
Death, on the living world of sense;
Because on my own land a shadow lies
That may not rise;
Because from bare grey hillside and rich city
Streams of uncomprehending sadness pour,

Thwarting the eager spirit's pure intelligence ...
How look (I muse) those cold and solitary stars
On these magnificent, cruel wars?

Stars trembled in broad heaven, faint with pity.
An hour to dawn I looked. Beside the trees
Wet mist shaped other trees that branching rose,
Covering the woods and putting out the stars.
There was no murmur on the seas,
No wind blew—only the wandering air that grows
With dawn, then murmurs, sighs,
And dies.
The mist climbed slowly, putting out the stars,
And the earth trembled when the stars were gone;
And moving strangely everywhere upon
The trembling earth, thickened the watery mist.

And for a time the holy things are veiled.
England's wise thoughts are swords; her quiet hours
Are trodden underfoot like wayside flowers,
And every English heart is England's wholly.
In starless night
A serious passion streams the heaven with light.
A common beating is in the air—
The heart of England throbbing everywhere.
And all her roads are nerves of noble thought,
And all her people's brain is but her brain;
And all her history, less her shame,
Is part of her requickened consciousness.
Her courage rises clean again.

Even in victory there hides defeat;
The spirit's murdered though the body survives,
Except the cause for which, a people strives
Burn with no covetous, foul heat.
Fights she against herself who infamously draws
The sword against man's secret spiritual laws.
But thou, England, because a bitter heel
Hath sought to bruise the brain, the sensitive will,
The conscience of the world,
For this, England, art risen, and shalt fight
Purely through long profoundest night,
Making their quarrel thine who are grieved like thee;
And (if to thee the stars yield victory)
Tempering their hate of the great foe that hurled
Vainly her strength against the conscience of the world.

I looked again, or dreamed I looked, and saw

The stars again and all their peace again.
The moving mist had gone, and shining still
The moon went high and pale above the hill.
Not now those lights were trembling in the vast
Ways of the nervy heaven, nor trembled earth:
Profound and calm they gazed as the soft-shod hours passed.
And with less fear (not with less awe,
Remembering, England, all the blood and pain)
How look, I cried, you stern and solitary stars
On these disastrous wars!

August, 1914.

SWEET ENGLAND

I heard a boy that climbed up Dover's Hill
Singing Sweet England, sweeter for his song.
The notes crept muffled through the copse, but still
Sharply recalled the things forgotten long,
The music that my own boy's lips had known,
Singing, and old airs on a wild flute blown;

And other hills, more grim and lonely far,
And valleys empty of these orchard trees;
A sheep-pond filled with the moon, a single star
I had watched by night searching the wreckful seas;
And all the streets and streets that childhood knew
In years when London streets were all my view.

And I remembered how that song I heard,
Sweet England, sung by children on May-day,
Nor any song was sweeter of a bird
Than that half-grievous air from children gay—
For then, as now, youth made the sadness bright,
Till the words, Sweet, Sweet England, shone with light.

Now, listening, I forgot how men yet fought
For this same England, till the song was done
And no sound lingered but the lark's, that brought
New music down from fields of cloud and sun,
Or the sad lapwing's over fields of green
Crying beneath the copse, near but unseen.

Then I remembered. All wide England spread
Before me, hill and wood and meadow and stream
And ancient roads and homes of men long dead,

And all the beauty a familiar dream.
On the green hills a cloud of silver grey
Gave gentle light stranger than light of day.

And clear between the hills, past the near crest
And many hills, the hungry cities crept,
Noble and mean, oppressive and oppressed,
Where dreams unrealized of England slept:
And they too England, packed in dusty street
With men that half forgot England was sweet.

Now men were far, but like a living brain
Quick with their thought, the earth, hills, air and light
Were quivering as though a shining rain
Falling all round made even the light more bright;
And trees and water and heath and hedge-flowers fair
With more than natural sweetness washed the air.

From hill to hill a sparkling web it swung,
A snare for happiness, lit with lovely dews.
The very smoke of cities now was hung
But like a grave girl's dress of tranquil hues:
And how (I thought) can England, seen thus bright,
Lifting her clear frank head, but love the light?—

No, not her brain! that bright web was the shadow
Of the high spirit in their spirit shining
Who on scarred foreign hill and trenchèd meadow
Kept the faith yet, unfearful, unrepining;—
Her faith that with the dark world's liberty
Mingles as earth's great rivers with the sea.

O with what gilding ray was the land agleam!
It was not sun and dew, bush, bough and leaf,
But human spirits visible as in a dream
That turns from glad to aching, being too brief:
Courage and beauty shining in such brightness
That all the thoughtful woods were no more lightless.

But most the hills a splendour had put on
Of golden honour, bright and high and calm
And like old heroes young men dream upon
When midnight stirs with magic sword and palm;—
With the fled mist all meanness put away
And the air clear and keen as salt sea-spray....

And yet no dream; no dream! I saw the whole,
The reap'd fields, idle kine and wandering sheep.

A weak wind through the near tall hedge-tree stole,
And died where Dover's Hill rose bare and steep;
I saw yet what I saw an hour ago,
But knew what save by dreams I did not know—

Sweet England!—wild proud heart of things unspoken
Spirit that men bear shyly and love purely;
That dies to live anew a life unbroken
As spring from every winter rising surely:
Sweet England unto generations sped,
Now bitter-sweetest for her daily dead.

September, 1916.

PRESAGE OF VICTORY

I

Then first I knew, seeing that bent grey head,
How England honours all her thousand dead.
Then first I knew how faith through black grief burns,
Until the ruined heart glows while it yearns
For one that never more returns—
Glows in the spent embers of its pride
For one that careless lived and fearless died.
And then I knew, then first,
How everywhere Hope from her prison had burst—
On every hill, wide dale, soft valley's lap,
In lonely cottage clutch'd between huge downs,
And streets confused with streets in clanging towns—
Like spring from winter's jail pouring her sap
Into the idle wood of last year's trees.
Then first I knew how the vast world-disease
Would die away, and England upon her seas
Shake every scab of sickness; toward new skies
Lifting a little holier her head,
With honesty the brighter in her eyes,
And all that urgent horror well forgot,
The dark remembered not;
Only remembered then, with bosom yet hot,
The blood that on how many a far field lies,
The bones enriching not our English earth
That brought them to such splendid birth
And the last sacrifice.

II

Then first I knew, seeing that head bent low,
How gravely all her days she needs must go,
Bearing an image in her faded breast....

O, the dark unrest
Of thoughts that never cease their flight,
Never vanishing, yet never still,
Like birds that wail round the bewildering nest!
But other nestlings never shall be hers,
Only a painful image his place fill,
Only a memory remain for her thin bosom to nurse
In all that dark unrest
Of sleepless and tormented night.

III

Yet from her eyes presage of victory
Looked steadfast out at mine.
It is not to be thought of (said her eyes)
That only a foul blotch the sun may shine
On England, through low poisonous thick skies!
Never, O never again
This pain, this pain!
Else from that foreign earth his bones would rise
And thrust in anger at the bitter skies.
It is not to be thought of that such prayer
Should fall unheeded back through heavy air.
But I have heard, in the night I have heard,
When not a leaf in all the orchard stirred,
And even the water of the bourne hung still,
And the old twitching, creaking house was still,
And all was still,
What was it I heard?
It could not be his voice, come from so far;
I know 'twas not a bird.
It was his voice, or that lone watchful star
Creeping above the casement bar,
Saying: Fear thou no ill,
No ill!
Then all the silence was an echoing round,
The water and dumb trees their antique murmur found,
And clear as music came the repeated Sound:
Fear thou no ill, no ill!

Was it her eyes or her tongue told me this?

IV

Yet but sad comfort from such pain is caught....
I went out from the house and climbed the coombe,
And where the first light of sweet morning hung
I found the light I sought.
From somewhere south a bugle's note was flung,
From somewhere north a sombre boom;
On the opposing hills white flecks and grey
Spotted the misty green,
And blue smoke wraiths around the tall trees clung.
Presently rose thick dust clouds from the green:
Came up, or seemed to come, the instant beat
Of marching feet;
Then with the clouds the beating died away,
And nothing was seen
But broken hills and the new flush of day.

V

All round the folding hills were like green waves,
Tossing awhile together ere they fall
And fling their salt on the steep stony beach.
The sound I heard was sound of Roman feet—
I saw the sparkling light on Roman glaives,
I heard the Roman speech
Answering the wild Iberian battle-call:
They passed from sight on the long street.
And I saw then the Mercian Kings that strode
Proudly from the small city of grey stone
And climbed the folding hills,
Past the full springs that bubbled and flowed
Through the soft valley and on to Avon stream.
They passed—as all things pass and seem
No other than a dream,
All but the shining and the echo gone.
But still I listened and looked. Their voice it was
Blown through the valley grass;
Their dust it was that sprang from the hard road
Where now these English legions flowed,
Waking the quiet like a steady wind.
That ancient soldiery before me passed
With all that followed them, and these the last
Of my own generation, my own mind;
Their strength and courage rooted deep in the earth
That brings men to such splendid birth
And no vain sacrifice ...
It was as when the land all darkness lies,
And shades, nor only shades, move freely out

And through the trees are heard and all about
Their ancient ways, 'neath the old stars and skies.
So now in morning's light I knew them there
Leading the men that marched and marched away,
And mounted up the hill, and down the hill
Passed from my eyes and ears, and left the air
Trembling everywhere,
And then how still!

VI

Then first I knew the joy that yet should be
Ringing from camped hill and guarded sea
With England's victory.
The dust had stirred, the infinite dust had stirred,
It was the courage of the past I heard,
The virtue of those buried bones again
Animate in these marching Englishmen;
And nothing wanted if the dead but nerved
The living hands that the same England served.
With new-washed eyes I saw as I went down
On the hill crest the oak-grove's crown,
With new delighted ear heard the lark sing—
That mad delighted thing;
The very smoke that rose was strangely blue,
But most the orchard brightened wonderfully new,
Where the wild spring, ere winter snow well gone,
Scattered her whiter, briefer snow-cloud down.
And England lovelier looked than when
Her dead roused not her living men.

May, 1916.

THE RETURN

I heard the rumbling guns. I saw the smoke,
The unintelligible shock of hosts that still,
Far off, unseeing, strove and strove again:
And Beauty flying naked down the hill.

From morn to eve: and then stern night cried Peace!
And shut the strife in darkness; all was still.
Then slowly crept a triumph on the dark—
And I heard Beauty singing up the hill.

ENGLISH HILLS

O that I were
Where breaks the pure cold light
On English hills,
And peewits rising cry,
And gray is all the sky.

Or at evening there
When the faint slow light stays,
And far below
Sleeps the last lingering sound,
And night leans all round.

O then, O there
'Tis English haunted ground.
The diligent stars
Creep out, watch, and smile;
The wise moon lingers awhile.

For surely there
Heroic shapes are moving,
Visible thoughts,
Passions, things divine,
Clear beneath clear star-shine.

O that I were
Again on English hills,
Seeing between
Laborious villages
Her cool dark loveliness.

HOMECOMING

When I came home from wanderings
In a tall chattering ship,
I thought a hundred happy things,
Of people, places, and such things
As I came sailing home.

The tall ship moved how slowly on
With me and hundreds more,
That thought not then of wanderings,
But of unwhispered, longed-for things,
Familiar things of home.

For not in miles seemed other lands
Far off, but in long years
As we came near to England then;
Even the tall ship heard secret things
As she moved trembling home.

It was at dawn. The chattering ship
Was strangely hushed; faint mist
Crept everywhere, and we crept on,
And every eye was creeping on
The mist, as we moved home....

Until we saw, far, very far,
Or dreamed we saw, her cliffs,
And thought of sweet, intolerable things,
Of England—dark, unwhispered things,
Such things, as we crept home.

ENGLAND'S ENEMY

She stands like one with mazy cares distraught.
Around her sudden angry storm-clouds rise,
Dark, dark! and comes the look into her eyes
Of eld. All that herself herself hath taught
She cons anew, that courage new be caught
Of courage old. Yet comfortless still lies
Snake-like in her warm bosom (vexed with sighs)
Fear of the greatness that herself hath wrought.

No glory but her memory teems with it,
No beauty that's not hers; more nobly none
Of all her sisters runs with her; but she
For her old destiny dreams herself unfit,
And fumbling at the future doubtfully
Muses how Rome of Romans was undone.

FROM PICCADILLY IN AUGUST

Now the trees rest: the moon has taught them sleep,
Like drowsy wings of bats are all their leaves,
Clinging together. Girls at ease who fold
Fair hands upon white necks and through dusk fields
Walk all content,—of them the trees have taken

Their way of evening rest; the yellow moon
With her pale gold has lit their dreams that lisp
On the wind's murmuring lips.
And low beyond
Burn those bright lamps beneath the moon more bright,
Lamps that but flash and sparkle and light not
The inward eye and musing thought, nor reach
Where, poplar-like, that tall-built campanile
Lifts to the neighbouring moon her head and feels
The pale gold like an ocean laving her.

EVENING BEAUTY: BLACKFRIARS

Nought is but beauty weareth, near and far,
Under the pale, blue sky and lonely star.
This is that quick hour when the city turns
Her troubled harsh distortion and blind care
Into brief loveliness seen everywhere,
While in the fuming west the low sun smouldering burns.

Not brick nor marble the rich beauty owns,
Not this is held in starward-pointing stones.
Sun, wind and smoke the threefold magic stir,
Kissing each favourless poor ruin with kiss
Like that when lovers lovers lure to bliss,
And earth than towered heaven awhile is heavenlier.

Tall shafts that show the sky how far away!
The thousand-window'd house gilded with day
That fades to night; the arches low, the streamer
Everywhere of the ruddy'd smoke.... Is aught
Of loveliness so rich e'er sold and bought?
Look visions fairer in the eyes of any dreamer?

Needs must so rare a beauty be so brief!
Night comes, of this delight the subtle thief.
Thou canst not, Night, this same rich thievery keep;
Seize it and look! 'tis gone, ere seized is gone—
Only in our warm bosoms lingering on,
A nest of precious dreams when our lids droop in sleep.

So in her darkening loveliness is she seen
Like an autumnal passion-haunted queen,
Who hears, "A captain-king is at the gate"—
"'Tis Antony, Antony!" Then hastens she,
Beauty to beauty adding yet, till—see,

A queen within the queen perilous with love and fate!

SAILING OF THE GLORY

Merrily shouted all the sailors
As they left the town behind;
Merrily shouted they and gladdened
At the slip-slap of the wind.
But envious were those faint home-keepers,
Faint land-lovers, as they saw
How the Glory dipped and staggered—
Envying saw
Pass the ship while all her sailors
Merrily shouted.

Far and far on eastern waters
Sailed the ship and yet sailed on,
While the townsmen, faint land-lovers,
Thought, "How long is't now she's gone?
Now, maybe, Bombay she touches,
Now strange craft about her throng";
Till she grew but half-remembered,
Gone so long:
Quite forgot how all her sailors
Merrily shouted.

Far in unfamiliar waters
Ship and shipmen harbourage found,
Where the rocks creep out like robbers
After travellers tempest-bound.
Then those faint land-lovers murmured
Doleful thanks not dead were they:—
Ah, yet envious, though the Glory
Sunken lay,
Hearing again those farewell voices
Merrily shouting.

AT THE DOCK

They loiter round the Dock that holds yon Ship
Shuddering at the dark pool's defiled lip
From springing bows to foam-deriding stern;
They have left her, and await her call "Return!"
Like any human mistress she has cast

Careless her ancient lovers, till at last
Perforce she calls them, and perforce they come
Like any human lovers.... Ah, what home
Know these, save in the Ship, the Ship! She groans
Day and night with travail of their strenuous bones.
They know her for their mother, sister, spouse,
Heart of their passion, idol of their vows;
They ward her, and she is their sure defence
'Gainst the sad waters' leagued malevolence.
The Ship, the Ship: they are her slaves, and she
Their Liege, their Faith, their Fate, their History.
Lo! they have bought her buoyancy with their blood
And their ribs cling the keel that cleaves the flood.
Their watches in the night, their loneliness,
Their toil, hunger and thirst, their heart's distress,
Their hands, their feet, far eye and smitten head
Whereon the Sea's upgathered weight is shed;
With these the Ship, the Ship is laid and rigged,
Launched and steered out; with these her living grave is digged,

They lean close over her—and long, perhaps,
For the broad seas and the loud wind that claps
Boisterous hands on the Ship's course; and wait
Her call who calls them with the voice of Fate.

"THE MEN WHO LOVED THE CAUSE THAT NEVER DIES"

O come you down from the far hills
Whereon you fought, triumphed and died,
Men at whose names the quick blood thrills
And the heart's troubled in our side.

Your shadows o'er our fields ere night
Draw from the shadow of old trees;
Ghost-hallowed run the streams, and light
Hangs halo-wise in the great peace.

Warriors of England whom we praise
(Ah, vain all praise!), your spirit is not
Lost in the meanness of these days,
Not wholly is your charge forgot.

And this perplexity of strife
Not all estrangèd leaves our heart;
England is ours yet, and her life
Has yet in ours the purest part.

But come you down and stand you yet
A little closer to our side,
Or in the darkness we forget
The cause for which Earth's noblest died.

JOHN FREEMAN – A CONCISE BIBLIOGRAPHY

Presage of Victory (1916)
Stone Trees (1916)
Ancient and Modern Essays in Literary Criticism (1917)
Memories of Childhood and other Poems (1919)
Poems 1909-1920 (1920)
Music (1921)
The Grove and Other Poems (1925)
Prince Absalom (1925)
Collected Poems (1928)
Last Poems (1930)

www.ingramcontent.com/pod-product-compliance
Lightning Source LLC
Chambersburg PA
CBHW072347090426
42741CB00012B/2949